Home Library

EDITOR: Maryanne Blacker

FOOD EDITOR: Pamela Clark

■ ■ ■

DEPUTY FOOD EDITOR: Barbara Northwood

ASSISTANT FOOD EDITOR: Jan Castorina

ASSOCIATE FOOD EDITOR: Enid Morrison

CO-ORDINATING EDITOR:
Jan Rudd

CHIEF HOME ECONOMIST: Karen Green

HOME ECONOMISTS: Jon Allen, Jane Ash,
Christine Chandler, Sue Hipwell, Karen Maughan,
Louise Patniotis, Jane Stone, Tania Thompson,
Kathy Wharton

EDITORIAL COORDINATOR: Elizabeth Hooper

KITCHEN ASSISTANT: Amy Wong

■ ■ ■

STYLISTS: Rosemary de Santis, Carolyn Fienberg,
Michelle Gorry, Jacqui Hing, Anna Phillips,
Belinda Warn

PHOTOGRAPHERS: Kevin Brown, Robert Clark,
Paul Clarke, Andre Martin, Georgia Moxham,
Robert Taylor

■ ■ ■

HOME LIBRARY STAFF:

ASSISTANT EDITOR: Bridget van Tinteren

ART DIRECTOR: Sue de Guingand

DESIGNER: Robbylee Phelan

EDITORIAL COORDINATOR: Fiona Lambrou

■ ■ ■

ACP PUBLISHER: Richard Walsh

ACP DEPUTY PUBLISHER: Nick Chan

■ ■ ■

Produced by The Australian Women's Weekly Home Library.
Typeset by ACP Color Graphics Pty Ltd.
Printed by Times Printers Pte. Ltd, Singapore.
Published by ACP Publishing Pty Ltd, 54 Park Street, Sydney.

♦ **U.S.A.:** Distributed for Whitecap Books Ltd by
Graphic Arts Center Publishing, 3019 N.W. Yeon,
Portland, OR, 97210. Tel: 503-226-2402. Fax: 530-223-1410.

♦ **CANADA:** Distributed in Canada by Whitecap
Books Ltd, 1086 West 3rd St,
North Vancouver B.C. V7P 3J6. Tel: 604- 980-9852.
Fax: 604-980-8197.

■ ■ ■

Starters and Soups
Includes index.
ISBN 1 863960 11 2

■ ■ ■

© A C P Publishing Pty Ltd 1994
ACN 053 273 546
This publication is copyright. No part of it may be reproduced
or transmitted in any form without the written permission
of the publishers.

■ ■ ■

COVER: Avocado and Artichoke Salad, page 12.
OPPOSITE: From left: Speedy Minestrone, Chunky Chorizo
Sausage and Bean Soup, page 120.
INSIDE BACK COVER: From top: Salmon and Fish Terrine
with Caper Mayonnaise; Lobster and Green Peppercorn Pate,
page 32.
BACK COVER: Double Potato Soup, page 103.

STARTERS AND SOUPS

Dinner party planning will be a fresh joy with our starters or appetizers and soups. Just one appetizer can precede the meal or several, plus dessert, can make a dinner with a difference. To plan a well-balanced menu, make sure you don't have similar ingredients and textures in courses. Many appetizers and soups are ideal for small meals or lunches. We have left seasoning with salt and pepper to the discretion of the cook.

Pamela Clark

FOOD EDITOR

Appetizers

Vegetables & Salads

Vegetables are tastiest if served as soon as they are cooked; they do not reheat well. Salads are best made just before serving; it is important to wash and thoroughly dry salad vegetables before using them.

Most dressings can be made up to 2 days ahead but are best made just before serving.

BELOW: Squash with Honey and
Gingerroot Vegetables.
RIGHT: Curried Vegetable Parcels.

SQUASH WITH HONEY AND GINGERROOT VEGETABLES

4 small golden nugget squash
4 teaspoons olive oil
½lb small yellow pattypan
**   squash, sliced**
1 carrot, sliced
1 onion, coarsely chopped
16 spears fresh asparagus, chopped

HONEY AND GINGERROOT GLAZE
½ cup honey
4 teaspoons grated fresh gingerroot
3 tablespoons fresh lemon juice
1 teaspoon curry powder

Cut a lid from each nugget squash, scoop out seeds. Brush inside and outside of squash lightly with oil, place squash on baking sheet, top with oiled lids. Bake in 350°F oven about 30 minutes or until squash are almost tender.

Boil, steam or microwave pattypan squash, carrot, onion and asparagus until tender; drain. Add hot glaze to vegetables; mix well. Spoon mixture into hot squash.
Honey and Gingerroot Glaze: Combine all ingredients in pan, stir over heat, without boiling, until combined.
Serves 4.

■ Squash can be cooked several hours ahead; reheat just before serving.
■ Storage: Covered, in refrigerator.
■ Freeze: Not suitable.
■ Microwave: Squash suitable.

2

CURRIED VEGETABLE PARCELS

2½oz broccoli, chopped
1 small carrot, sliced
1 small zucchini, sliced
1 tablespoon butter
1 onion, finely chopped
1 clove garlic, minced
1 teaspoon curry powder
1 teaspoon all-purpose flour
⅓ cup canned unsweetened coconut cream
¼ cup water
4 teaspoons dark seedless raisins
8 sheets phyllo pastry
2 tablespoons (¼ stick) butter, extra

CILANTRO HOLLANDAISE
¼ cup white vinegar
2 fresh parsley stems
1 bay leaf
2 egg yolks
½ cup (1 stick) butter, chopped
4 teaspoons chopped fresh cilantro

Boil, steam or microwave broccoli, carrot and zucchini until tender; drain. Heat butter in pan, add onion and garlic, cook, stirring, until onion is soft.

Add curry powder and flour, cook, stirring, 1 minute. Remove from heat, stir in coconut cream and water, stir over high heat until sauce boils and thickens. Stir in vegetables and raisins; cool.

Layer 2 pastry sheets together, brushing each with extra butter, fold in half. Place one-quarter of vegetable mixture onto pastry, tuck ends in, roll pastry up; place on baking sheet. Repeat with remaining pastry, extra butter and vegetable mixture. Lightly brush parcels with butter, bake in 350°F oven about 25 minutes or until lightly browned. Spoon hollandaise evenly over parcels, broil about 2 minutes or until lightly browned.

Cilantro Hollandaise: Combine vinegar, parsley and bay leaf in pan. Simmer, uncovered, until liquid is reduced to about 3 tablespoons, strain, reserve liquid; cool to room temperature.

Combine egg yolks and vinegar mixture in heatproof bowl over simmering water. Whisk until slightly thickened, gradually whisk in butter over heat, whisk until thick; stir in cilantro.

Serves 4.

- Filling can be made 2 days ahead.
- Storage: Covered, in refrigerator.
- Freeze: Not suitable.
- Microwave: Filling suitable.

3

EGGPLANT TAHINI DIP

1 eggplant, sliced
¼ cup tahini (sesame paste)
¼ cup fresh lemon juice
⅓ cup olive oil
1 clove garlic, minced
4 teaspoons tomato paste
1 small green bell pepper, chopped
4 teaspoons chopped fresh mint

Place eggplant on baking sheet in single layer. Bake in 400°F oven about 15 minutes, turning occasionally, or until soft. Remove skin from eggplant; blend or process eggplant with tahini, juice, oil, garlic and tomato paste until smooth. Stir in pepper, place in dish; cover, refrigerate until cold. Sprinkle with mint just before serving. Serve with fresh vegetables or crackers.

Serves 4.

- Dip can be made a day ahead.
- Storage: Covered, in refrigerator.
- Freeze: Not suitable.
- Microwave: Suitable.

BROCCIFLOWER FRITTERS WITH ROQUEFORT SAUCE

7oz cauliflower, chopped
5oz broccoli, chopped
oil for deep-frying

BATTER
1 egg
4 teaspoons light olive oil
1 cup water
1 cup all-purpose flour

ROQUEFORT SAUCE
2⅓ cups heavy cream
3 green onions, chopped
1 clove garlic, minced
2 tablespoons (¼ stick) butter
3 tablespoons all-purpose flour
3½oz Roquefort cheese, crumbled

Boil, steam or microwave cauliflower and broccoli until just tender; drain. Dip vegetables into batter, deep-fry in batches in hot oil until lightly browned; drain on absorbent paper. Serve fritters hot with sauce.

Batter: Combine egg, oil and water in bowl, whisk until combined. Whisk in sifted flour in several batches, whisk until smooth (or blend or process all ingredients until smooth).

Roquefort Sauce: Combine cream, onions and garlic in pan, simmer, uncovered, about 15 minutes or until mixture is reduced by about half. Melt butter in separate pan, stir in flour, cook, stirring, 1 minute. Remove from heat, gradually stir in cream mixture, stir over high heat until sauce boils and thickens; cool 5 minutes. Transfer sauce to blender or processor, add cheese, blend until smooth. Reheat without boiling.

Serves 4.

- Deep-fry vegetables just before serving.
- Freeze: Not suitable.
- Microwave: Vegetables suitable.

CORN HUSKS WITH VEGETABLE FILLING

4 ears corn in husks
3 tablespoons olive oil
1 clove garlic, minced
1 small green bell pepper, chopped
1 small red bell pepper, chopped
1 small onion, chopped
1 small zucchini, chopped
3½oz button mushrooms, sliced

LIGHT CHEESE SAUCE
2 tablespoons (¼ stick) butter
4 teaspoons all-purpose flour
⅔ cup milk
⅔ cup heavy cream
½ cup grated cheddar cheese
3 tablespoons chopped fresh chives

Remove corn carefully from husks, keeping husks intact at base. Remove silk from corn, remove kernels.

Heat oil in skillet, add garlic, cook, stirring, until fragrant. Add all vegetables, cook, stirring, about 2 minutes or until tender; cool.

Trim ends from husks, fill with vegetable mixture, tie husks together with a strip of husk. Place filled husks into large steamer, steam, covered, about 20 minutes or until heated through. Serve with light cheese sauce.

Light Cheese Sauce: Melt butter in pan, add flour, cook, stirring, 1 minute. Remove from heat, gradually stir in milk and cream, stir over high heat until mixture boils and thickens. Stir in cheese and chives.

Serves 4.

- Recipe can be prepared several hours ahead; steam filled husks just before serving. Sauce best made close to serving.
- Storage: Covered, in refrigerator.
- Freeze: Not suitable.
- Microwave: Suitable.

PUMPKIN SQUASH AND CELERY AU GRATIN

10oz pumpkin squash, chopped
2 tablespoons (¼ stick) butter
1 clove garlic, minced
1 stalk celery, sliced
3 tablespoons all-purpose flour
⅛ teaspoon ground nutmeg
¼ cup water
¾ cup heavy cream
3 tablespoons grated Parmesan cheese

TOPPING
1 cup fresh bread crumbs
2 tablespoons (¼ stick) butter, melted
¼ cup grated Parmesan cheese

Boil, steam or microwave squash until tender; drain. Melt butter in pan, add garlic and celery, cook, stirring, until celery is just tender.

Add flour and nutmeg, stir until dry and grainy. Remove from heat, gradually stir in combined water and cream, stir over heat until mixture boils and thickens. Remove from heat; stir in cheese and squash.

Spoon mixture into 4 ovenproof dishes (1 cup capacity), sprinkle evenly with topping. Bake in 375°F oven about 15 minutes or until lightly browned.

Topping: Combine all ingredients in bowl.

Serves 4.

- Recipe can be prepared several hours ahead; bake just before serving.
- Storage: Covered, in refrigerator.
- Freeze: Not suitable.
- Microwave: Filling suitable.

WARM VEGETABLE RIBBONS WITH CHILI PLUM GLAZE

2 large zucchini
2 large carrots
2 large parsnips
4 teaspoons sesame seeds, toasted

CHILI PLUM GLAZE
¼ teaspoon Oriental sesame oil
1 clove garlic, minced
¼ cup plum sauce
1 teaspoon light soy sauce
1 teaspoon chili sauce
4 teaspoons water

Cut zucchini, carrots and parsnips into 3 inch lengths. Carefully peel strips from each piece using vegetable peeler. Steam or microwave vegetable until just tender; drain well. Combine vegetable ribbons and glaze in large bowl, sprinkle with sesame seeds.

Chili Plum Glaze: Combine oil, garlic, sauces and water in pan, stir over heat until heated through.

Serves 4.

- Vegetables can be prepared several hours ahead; cook just before serving.
- Storage: Uncooked vegetable ribbons, covered with water, in bowl.
- Freeze: Not suitable.
- Microwave: Suitable.

ABOVE: Clockwise from top: Corn Husks with Vegetable Filling; Warm Vegetable Ribbons with Chili Plum Glaze; Pumpkin Squash and Celery au Gratin.
LEFT: From top: Brocciflower Fritters with Roquefort Sauce; Eggplant Tahini Dip.

PASTA WITH ZUCCHINI AND MINT SAUCE

3oz (¾ stick) butter
3 medium zucchini, grated
8oz package cream cheese
⅓ cup grated Parmesan cheese
⅓ cup milk
1 clove garlic, minced
½ cup fresh mint sprigs
½lb fresh pasta

Heat butter in skillet, add zucchini, cook, stirring, until just soft. Blend or process cheeses, milk, garlic and mint until smooth. Add to zucchini mixture, stir gently until heated through. Add pasta to large pan of boiling water, boil, uncovered, until just tender; drain. Return to pan, gently stir in zucchini mixture. Serve with extra Parmesan cheese, if desired.

Serves 4.

■ Recipe best made just before serving.
■ Freeze: Not suitable.
■ Microwave: Not suitable.

ARTICHOKES WITH WARM PEPPERY VINAIGRETTE

2 globe artichokes
3 tablespoons fresh lemon juice

PEPPERY VINAIGRETTE
1 small red bell pepper, sliced
⅓ cup olive oil
⅓ cup salad oil
3 tablespoons white wine vinegar
3 tablespoons fresh lemon juice
1 teaspoon cracked black peppercorns
½ teaspoon sugar

Trim stems from artichokes, discard any tough outside leaves, shorten outside leaf tips with scissors. Add juice to large pan of boiling water. Add artichokes, simmer, covered, about 30 minutes or until tender. Drain well, cut artichokes in half, serve with peppery vinaigrette.
Peppery Vinaigrette: Add bell pepper to small pan of boiling water; drain immediately. Combine bell pepper with remaining ingredients in pan, heat without boiling.

Serves 4.

■ Recipe best made just before serving.
■ Freeze: Not suitable.
■ Microwave: Vinaigrette suitable.

FRESH ASPARAGUS WITH STRAWBERRY VINAIGRETTE

We used a leek leaf to tie asparagus together. Cut leaf into 4 thin strips about 7 inches long, boil or steam until just tender. Asparagus bundles can also be tied with chives.

1lb fresh asparagus

STRAWBERRY VINAIGRETTE
¼lb strawberries
1 teaspoon grated orange zest
3 tablespoons cider vinegar
¼ cup salad oil

Boil, steam or microwave asparagus until just tender; drain. Rinse under cold water; drain. Tie bundles of asparagus together, serve with strawberry vinaigrette.
Strawberry Vinaigrette: Blend strawberries until smooth, transfer to small bowl, whisk in zest, vinegar and oil.

Serves 4.

■ Recipe can be made several hours ahead.
■ Storage: Covered, at room temperature.
■ Freeze: Not suitable.
■ Microwave: Suitable.

ABOVE: Pasta with Zucchini and Mint Sauce.
RIGHT: From top: Fresh Asparagus with Strawberry Vinaigrette; Artichokes with Warm Peppery Vinaigrette.

ZUCCHINI MOUSSES WITH PARMESAN SAUCE

¼ cup (½ stick) butter
1 clove garlic, minced
7oz zucchini, chopped
2 green onions, chopped
3 tablespoons all-purpose flour
⅔ cup milk
1 tablespoon unflavored gelatin
3 tablespoons water
½ cup whipping cream

PARMESAN SAUCE
⅔ cup heavy cream
½ cup grated Parmesan cheese
1 egg, lightly beaten

Lightly oil 6 molds (⅓ cup capacity). Melt butter in pan, add garlic, zucchini and onions, cook, stirring, until zucchini are tender. Stir in flour, cook, stirring, 1 minute. Remove from heat, gradually stir in milk, stir over high heat until mixture boils and thickens. Blend or process zucchini mixture until smooth; cool.

Sprinkle gelatin over water in cup, stand in small pan of simmering water, stir until dissolved; stir into zucchini mixture. Beat cream in small bowl until soft peaks form, fold into zucchini mixture. Spoon mixture into prepared molds, cover; refrigerate several hours or overnight. Turn mousses out, serve with sauce.
Parmesan Sauce: Add cream to small pan, bring to boil, stir in cheese. Remove from heat, stir in egg. Stir over heat until slightly thickened; do not boil. Serve at room temperature.

Serves 6.

- Mousses can be made a day ahead. Sauce best made just before serving.
- Storage: Covered, in refrigerator.
- Freeze: Not suitable.
- Microwave: Mousses suitable.

CABBAGE AND ONION WITH HOT PEPPER DRESSING

3 tablespoons olive oil
2 cups coarsely shredded red cabbage
2 cups coarsely shredded white cabbage
1 onion, sliced
1 red bell pepper, sliced

HOT PEPPER DRESSING
¼ cup white wine vinegar
⅓ cup olive oil
1 teaspoon cracked black peppercorns
1 clove garlic, minced
½ teaspoon sambal oelek
4 teaspoons chopped fresh parsley

Heat oil in wok or skillet, add cabbage, onion and pepper, stir-fry about 2 minutes or until vegetables are just starting to wilt. Add dressing, stir until combined.
Hot Pepper Dressing: Combine all ingredients in jar; shake well.

Serves 6.

- Recipe best made just before serving.
- Freeze: Not suitable.
- Microwave: Suitable.

ABOVE: Cabbage and Onion with Hot Pepper Dressing.
LEFT: Zucchini Mousse with Parmesan Sauce.

LEEKS IN ORANGE VINAIGRETTE

4 small leeks
1 orange

ORANGE VINAIGRETTE
½ cup salad oil
4 teaspoons white wine vinegar
2 teaspoons grated orange zest
3 tablespoons fresh orange juice
1 clove garlic, minced
2 teaspoons chopped fresh tarragon

Cut leeks diagonally into 1¼ inch pieces. Boil, steam or microwave leeks until tender; cool. Cut peel thinly from orange, cut peel into fine strips. Serve leeks with orange vinaigrette and peel strips.
Orange Vinaigrette: Combine all ingredients in jar; shake well.

Serves 4.

- Recipe can be prepared several hours ahead.
- Storage: Covered, in refrigerator.
- Freeze: Not suitable.
- Microwave: Suitable.

MARINATED RED BELL PEPPERS

4 large red bell peppers
3 cloves garlic, minced
3 tablespoons chopped fresh oregano
1 cup olive oil

Quarter peppers lengthways, remove seeds. Broil peppers skin-side-up until skin blisters and blackens. Wrap peppers in clean cloth, stand 5 minutes, peel away skin. Cut peppers into strips. Combine peppers, garlic, oregano and oil in bowl, cover; refrigerate overnight. Serve with crusty bread.

Serves 4.

- Recipe can be made a month ahead.
- Storage: Covered, in refrigerator.
- Freeze: Not suitable.
- Microwave: Not suitable.

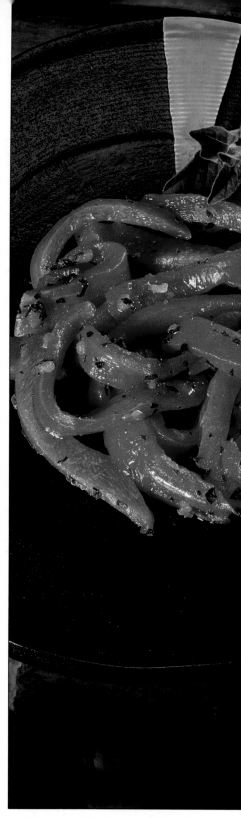

MUSTARD SEED EGGPLANT WITH TOMATO RELISH

2 medium eggplants, sliced
coarse (kosher) salt
½ cup all-purpose flour
1 egg, separated
¾ cup water
3 tablespoons olive oil
2 teaspoons seeded mustard
oil for shallow-frying

TOMATO RELISH

4 large tomatoes, peeled, chopped
1 large onion, chopped
¾ cup turbinado sugar
¾ cup cider vinegar
1 apple, chopped
½ cup golden raisins
1 clove garlic, minced
1 teaspoon sambal oelek
1 teaspoon seeded mustard
½ teaspoon ground cumin

Place eggplant in large colander, sprinkle with salt, stand 20 minutes. Rinse eggplant under cold water, drain well on absorbent paper.

Sift flour into large bowl, gradually stir in combined egg yolk, water, oil and mustard, stir until smooth. Beat egg white in small bowl until soft peaks form, fold into batter.

Dip eggplant into batter, shallow-fry in hot oil until browned; drain on absorbent paper. Serve with tomato relish.

Tomato Relish: Combine all ingredients in large pan, stir over heat, without boiling, until sugar is dissolved. Boil, uncovered, without stirring, about 30 minutes or until slightly thickened.

Serves 4.

- Shallow-fry eggplant just before serving. Relish can be made a month ahead.
- Storage: Relish, covered, in refrigerator.
- Freeze: Not suitable.
- Microwave: Not suitable.

ABOVE: From left: Marinated Red Bell Peppers; Mustard Seed Eggplant with Tomato Relish.
LEFT: Leeks in Orange Vinaigrette.

SPINACH SALAD ON CRUNCHY CROUTES

3 slices bacon, chopped
3 tablespoons olive oil
1 clove garlic, minced
4 thick slices white Vienna loaf
1 bunch (1¼lb) spinach, chopped
¼ cup sesame seeds, toasted
3 tablespoons grated Parmesan
    cheese

DRESSING
¼ cup olive oil
¼ cup fresh lemon juice
4 teaspoons Oriental sesame oil
2 teaspoons light soy sauce
1 teaspoon sugar

Add bacon to skillet, cook, stirring, until crisp; drain on absorbent paper. Heat oil in skillet, add garlic, cook, stirring, until fragrant. Add bread, cook until crisp and golden on both sides; cool. Combine spinach, seeds and bacon in bowl, toss in warm dressing. Serve croutes topped with spinach salad and cheese.
Dressing: Combine all ingredients in pan; heat until just warm.

Serves 4.

■ Croutes can be made a day ahead. Salad best made just before serving.
■ Storage: In airtight container.
■ Freeze: Not suitable.
■ Microwave: Not suitable.

AVOCADO AND ARTICHOKE SALAD

1 avocado, sliced
8 bottled artichoke hearts in oil,
    quartered
2 small green cucumbers, sliced
1 small red leaf lettuce

LIME AND BASIL VINAIGRETTE
¼ cup olive oil
¼ cup fresh lime juice
1 small fresh red chili pepper,
    finely chopped
4 teaspoons chopped fresh basil
½ teaspoon superfine sugar

Combine avocado, artichokes and cucumbers in bowl, add dressing, cover, refrigerate several hours. Serve salad over lettuce.
Lime and Basil Vinaigrette: Combine all ingredients in jar; shake well.

Serves 4.

■ Recipe best prepared several hours ahead.
■ Storage: Covered, in refrigerator.
■ Freeze: Not suitable.

RIGHT: Avocado and Artichoke Salad.
ABOVE: Spinach Salad on Crunchy Croutes.

BRAISED BELL PEPPERS WITH SOUFFLE TOPPING

unseasoned packaged bread crumbs
4 teaspoons olive oil
1 onion, chopped
1 clove garlic, minced
1 red bell pepper, sliced
1 green bell pepper, sliced
5 tomatoes, peeled, chopped
4 teaspoons tomato paste

CHEESE SOUFFLE TOPPING
2 tablespoons (¼ stick) butter
4 teaspoons all-purpose flour
1 cup milk
¼ cup grated cheddar cheese
2 eggs, separated

Grease inside top half of 4 ovenproof dishes (1 cup capacity), sprinkle greased area with bread crumbs; shake away excess crumbs.

Heat oil in skillet, add onion and garlic, cook, stirring, until lightly browned. Add peppers, cook, stirring, further 2 minutes. Stir in tomatoes and tomato paste, simmer, covered, 20 minutes. Pour into prepared dishes, place dishes on baking sheet. Divide souffle mixture evenly over peppers. Bake in 375°F oven about 25 minutes or until lightly browned.

Cheese Souffle Topping: Melt butter in pan, stir in flour, cook, stirring, 1 minute. Remove from heat, gradually stir in milk, stir over high heat until mixture boils and thickens; stir in cheese. Cool 5 minutes, stir in egg yolks. Beat egg whites in small bowl with electric mixer until soft peaks form, fold into cheese mixture in 2 batches.

Serves 4.

- ■ Recipe best made just before serving.
- ■ Freeze: Not suitable.
- ■ Microwave: Not suitable.

MINT, MELON AND CANTALOUPE COCKTAIL

1 honeydew melon
¼ small watermelon
1 cantaloupe
3 tablespoons chopped fresh mint
¼ cup fresh lime juice

Cut shapes from slices of melons and cantaloupe or scoop into balls using melon baller, combine with mint and juice in bowl. Cover, refrigerate at least 1 hour before serving.

Serves 6 to 8.

- ■ Cocktail can be made several hours ahead.
- ■ Storage: Covered, in refrigerator.
- ■ Freeze: Not suitable.

RIGHT: Mint, Melon and Cantaloupe Cocktail.
LEFT: From top: Braised Bell Peppers with Souffle Topping; Fresh Pea Souffles with Mint Sauce.

FRESH PEA SOUFFLES WITH MINT SAUCE

unseasoned packaged bread crumbs
2 tablespoons (¼ stick) butter
1 small onion, finely chopped
1 teaspoon superfine sugar
3 tablespoons water
1 cup (¼lb) frozen green peas
¼ cup (½ stick) butter, extra
3 tablespoons all-purpose flour
1 cup milk
3 egg yolks, lightly beaten
4 egg whites

MINT SAUCE
2 tablespoons (¼ stick) butter
4 teaspoons all-purpose flour
1¼ cups milk
1 teaspoon fresh lemon juice
4 teaspoons chopped fresh mint

Grease 8 ovenproof dishes (½ cup capacity), sprinkle evenly with bread crumbs. Heat butter in pan, add onion, cook, stirring, until soft. Add sugar, water and peas, simmer, uncovered, until peas are tender. Blend, process or sieve pea mixture until smooth.

Heat extra butter in pan, stir in flour, cook, stirring, 1 minute. Remove from heat, gradually stir in milk, stir over high heat until mixture boils and thickens.

Pour mixture into bowl; cool. Stir in pea mixture and egg yolks. Beat egg whites in bowl with electric mixer until soft peaks form. Lightly fold into pea mixture in 2 batches. Place prepared dishes on baking sheet, evenly spoon in pea mixture. Bake in 400°F oven 10 minutes, reduce heat to 350°F, bake further 5 minutes or until golden brown. Serve with mint sauce.

Mint Sauce: Melt butter in pan, stir in flour, cook, stirring, 1 minute. Remove from heat, gradually stir in milk and juice, stir over high heat until mixture boils and thickens; stir in mint.

Serves 8.

- ■ Make souffles just before serving. Sauce can be made an hour ahead; add mint after reheating.
- ■ Storage: Covered, in refrigerator.
- ■ Freeze: Not suitable.
- ■ Microwave: Souffle mixture and sauce suitable.

WARM MUSHROOM AND WATERCRESS SALAD

½ cup olive oil
¼ cup water
½ cup fresh lemon juice
½ teaspoon superfine sugar
1 small red bell pepper,
    finely chopped
3 tablespoons chopped fresh oregano
½lb button mushrooms
1 small radicchio lettuce
1½ cups watercress sprigs

Combine oil, water, juice, sugar, pepper and oregano in bowl. Stir in mushrooms, cover, refrigerate several hours or overnight. Transfer mixture to pan, stir over low heat without boiling until heated through. Combine mixture with lettuce and watercress in bowl.

Serves 4.

■ Recipe can be made a day ahead.
■ Storage: Covered, in refrigerator.
■ Freeze: Not suitable.
■ Microwave: Not suitable.

BELOW: Spinach and Bean Lasagne.
LEFT: Warm Mushroom and
Watercress Salad.
RIGHT: Orange Watercress Salad.

SPINACH AND BEAN LASAGNE

½lb lasagne sheets
½lb ricotta cheese
⅓ cup grated Parmesan cheese
¼ cup heavy cream

BEAN FILLING
1 tablespoon butter
1 clove garlic, minced
1 red bell pepper, chopped
19oz can white kidney beans
    (cannellini), drained
3 tablespoons sour cream
3 tablespoons tomato paste
1 egg

SPINACH FILLING
1 tablespoon butter
8 large spinach leaves, chopped
½lb ricotta cheese
¼ teaspoon ground nutmeg

Cook 3 to 4 lasagne sheets at a time, depending on size of pan. Add lasagne sheets gradually to large pan of boiling water, boil, uncovered, until just tender. Remove lasagne from pan, place in large bowl of cold water, drain well before using. Cover base of 7 inch x 10 inch ovenproof dish with a layer of lasagne, spread evenly with half the bean filling. Top with a layer of lasagne, spread evenly with all spinach filling. Top with lasagne, remaining bean filling and finally the remaining lasagne.

Beat cheeses and cream in small bowl, spread mixture evenly over lasagne. Bake in 350°F oven about 30 minutes or until golden brown.

Bean Filling: Melt butter in pan, add garlic and pepper, cook, stirring, until pepper is just soft. Process mixture with remaining ingredients until combined.

Spinach Filling: Melt butter in pan, add spinach, cook, stirring, until spinach is tender and liquid evaporated, drain spinach well; cool 5 minutes. Stir in cheese and nutmeg.

Serves 4 to 6.

- Recipe can be prepared a day ahead. Cook lasagne just before serving.
- Storage: Covered, in refrigerator.
- Freeze: Not suitable.
- Microwave: Fillings suitable.

ORANGE WATERCRESS SALAD

1 large onion, thinly sliced
3 large oranges, thickly sliced
2 cups watercress sprigs
18 pitted black olives

MUSTARD DRESSING
⅓ cup olive oil
½ teaspoon dry mustard
¼ teaspoon superfine sugar
¼ cup white wine vinegar

Add onion to small pan of boiling water, boil 30 seconds; drain. Rinse under cold water; drain. Combine onion, oranges, watercress, olives and dressing in bowl.

Mustard Dressing: Combine all ingredients in jar; shake well.

Serves 6.

- Recipe best made just before serving.
- Freeze: Not suitable.
- Microwave: Not suitable.

CARROT AND CHIVE SOUFFLES

2 carrots, chopped
¼ cup (½ stick) butter
3 tablespoons all-purpose flour
¾ cup milk
3 eggs, separated
3 tablespoons chopped fresh chives

LEMON SOUR CREAM
⅓ cup sour cream
3 tablespoons heavy cream
1 teaspoon grated lemon zest

Boil, steam or microwave carrots until tender; drain. Blend, process or push carrots through sieve. You will need about ½ cup puree for this recipe.

Melt butter in pan, stir in flour, cook, stirring, 1 minute. Remove from heat, gradually stir in milk, stir over high heat until mixture boils and thickens. Remove mixture from heat, quickly stir in beaten egg yolks, carrot puree and chives.

Beat egg whites until firm peaks form, fold into carrot mixture in 2 batches. Spoon mixture evenly into 6 greased souffle dishes (¾ cup capacity), bake in 375°F oven about 20 minutes or until lightly browned. Serve with lemon sour cream.

Lemon Sour Cream: Combine all ingredients in bowl.

Serves 6.

■ Make souffles just before serving. Lemon sour cream can be made several hours ahead.
■ Storage: Covered, in refrigerator.
■ Freeze: Not suitable.
■ Microwave: Souffle mixture suitable.

CREPE ROULADE WITH PUMPKIN SQUASH FILLING

You will need to cook about 3lb pumpkin squash for this recipe. You will need a 20 inch square of calico, washed and dried, to make roulade.

½ cup all-purpose flour
2 eggs, lightly beaten
⅔ cup milk

PUMPKIN SQUASH FILLING
2 tablespoons (¼ stick) butter
4 teaspoons all-purpose flour
¼ cup milk
¾ cup grated cheddar cheese
2 cups mashed pumpkin squash
2 eggs, lightly beaten
1 egg white
½ teaspoon ground nutmeg
3 tablespoons chopped fresh chives

Sift flour into bowl, gradually stir in combined eggs and milk, mix to a smooth batter (or blend or process all ingredients until smooth). Cover, stand 30 minutes. Pour 3 to 4 tablespoons of batter into heated greased 9 inch crepe pan, cook until lightly browned underneath. Turn crepe, cook other side. Repeat with remaining batter. You will need 6 crepes slightly overlapping on calico as shown.

Spread crepes evenly with pumpkin squash mixture.

Roll crepes from long side like a jelly-roll, using the calico to lift and guide the roulade carefully.

Wrap calico firmly around roulade, secure ends tightly with kitchen string.

Lower roulade gently into large pan of boiling water (the pan should be about two-thirds full of water), cover, boil 15 minutes. Carefully lift roulade from water to plate; cool. Refrigerate overnight. Cut string, carefully remove calico. Slice roulade just before serving.

Pumpkin Squash Filling: Melt butter in pan, stir in flour, cook, stirring, 1 minute. Remove from heat, gradually stir in milk, stir over high heat until mixture boils and thickens. Stir in cheese and squash, then eggs, egg white, nutmeg and chives; cool.

Serves 6.

- Recipe best made a day ahead.
- Storage: Covered, in refrigerator.
- Freeze: Not suitable.
- Microwave: Not suitable.

ABOVE: Carrot and Chive Souffles.
LEFT: Crepe Roulade with Pumpkin Squash Filling.

19

CARROT SOUFFLE CREPES WITH FRESH HERB BUTTER

2 carrots, chopped
2 eggs, separated
4 teaspoons heavy cream
3 tablespoons grated Parmesan cheese
¼ teaspoon ground cumin

CREPES
½ cup all-purpose flour
2 eggs, lightly beaten
¾ cup milk
2 teaspoons light olive oil

FRESH HERB BUTTER
½ cup (1 stick) butter, chopped
3 tablespoons chopped fresh parsley
4 teaspoons chopped fresh chives
1 teaspoon chopped fresh thyme

Boil, steam or microwave carrots until tender; drain. Blend, process or push through sieve. You will need ½ cup pureed carrot.

Combine carrot puree, egg yolks, cream, cheese and cumin in bowl. Beat egg whites with electric mixer until soft peaks form, fold into carrot mixture.

Divide mixture evenly over crepes, fold crepes in half, then half again to form triangles. Place triangles in single layer on greased baking sheet, bake in 350°F oven about 15 minutes or until puffed. Serve crepes immediately with herb butter.

Crepes: Sift flour into bowl, gradually stir in combined eggs, milk and oil, mix to a smooth batter (or blend or process all ingredients until smooth). Cover, stand 30 minutes. Pour 3 to 4 tablespoons of batter into heated greased crepe pan; cook until lightly browned underneath. Turn crepe, brown on other side. Repeat with remaining batter. You will need 8 crepes.

Fresh Herb Butter: Beat ingredients together in bowl with electric mixer, spoon onto sheet of baking paper in log shape, roll up firmly; refrigerate until firm.

Serves 4.

- Cook completed crepes just before serving. Unfilled crepes can be made 2 days ahead. Herb butter can be made a week ahead.
- Storage: Crepes, layered with paper, in refrigerator. Butter, in refrigerator.
- Freeze: Unfilled crepes and butter suitable.
- Microwave: Not suitable.

CHERRY TOMATO AND SUGAR SNAP PEA SALAD

½lb sugar snap peas
½lb cherry tomatoes

ORANGE DRESSING
¼ cup salad oil
4 teaspoons white wine vinegar
1 teaspoon coarsely grated orange zest
4 teaspoons fresh orange juice
½ teaspoon sugar

Boil, steam or microwave peas until just tender, rinse under cold water; drain. Combine peas and tomatoes in bowl, add dressing; toss well.

Orange Dressing: Combine all ingredients in jar; shake well.

Serves 4.

- Recipe can be made several hours ahead.
- Storage: Covered, in refrigerator.
- Freeze: Not suitable.
- Microwave: Peas suitable.

BELOW: Carrot Souffle Crepes with Fresh Herb Butter.
RIGHT: Cherry Tomato and Sugar Snap Pea Salad.

CREAMY PASTA WITH SPINACH AND BACON

7oz fresh white pasta
7oz fresh green pasta
4 slices bacon, chopped
2 cloves garlic, minced
8 large spinach leaves, chopped
½ teaspoon ground nutmeg
½ cup heavy cream
¼ cup grated Parmesan cheese

Add pasta gradually to large pan of boiling water, boil, uncovered, until just tender; drain well.

Add bacon and garlic to pan, cook, stirring, until bacon is crisp. Stir in spinach, cook, covered, over high heat about 2 minutes or until spinach is just wilted. Reduce heat, stir in nutmeg and cream, then pasta. Serve sprinkled with cheese.

Serves 6.

■ Recipe best made just
  before serving.
■ Freeze: Not suitable.
■ Microwave: Not suitable.

PASTA WITH CREAMY BASIL AND ALMOND SAUCE

½lb pasta
1 cup fresh basil leaves, chopped
½ cup (1 stick) butter, chopped
3 tablespoons heavy cream
⅓ cup slivered almonds, toasted

Add pasta gradually to large pan of boiling water, boil, uncovered, until just tender; drain. Return pasta to pan, gently stir in basil, butter, cream and almonds.

Serves 4.

■ Recipe best made just
  before serving.
■ Freeze: Not suitable.
■ Microwave: Not suitable.

COCONUT RICE IN LETTUCE ROLLS

You will need to cook ⅔ cup rice for this recipe; we used Basmati rice.

4 teaspoons light olive oil
½ cup pine nuts
**1 small red bell pepper,
    finely chopped**
4 teaspoons grated fresh gingerroot
2 cups cooked rice
3½oz snow peas, sliced
**⅓ cup canned unsweetened
    coconut milk**
3 tablespoons fresh lime juice
4 large lettuce leaves

Heat oil in wok or skillet. Add pine nuts, pepper and gingerroot, stir-fry until nuts are lightly browned. Stir in rice and peas, stir-fry until heated through. Stir in combined coconut milk and juice; stir-fry about 2 minutes or until heated through. Serve rice mixture rolled in lettuce leaves.

Serves 4.

■ Recipe best made just before serving.
■ Freeze: Not suitable.
■ Microwave: Not suitable.

RICOTTA, CHICKEN AND SPINACH QUENELLES

½ bunch (10oz) spinach
½ cup heavy cream
2 small boneless, skinless chicken
    breast halves
¼lb ricotta cheese
3 egg whites

TOMATO ONION SAUCE
4 teaspoons olive oil
1 clove garlic, minced
1 small onion, chopped
4 teaspoons tomato paste
14½oz can tomatoes
½ teaspoon superfine sugar

Steam, boil or microwave spinach until just tender; drain, rinse under cold water, drain well.

Blend or process spinach and cream until smooth, transfer mixture to large bowl. Process chicken, cheese and egg whites until smooth, stir into spinach mixture. Spread mixture evenly onto large flat plate or tray, refrigerate several hours or overnight until firm.

Mold mixture into oval shapes, using 2 wet dessertspoons. Place ovals carefully into large shallow pan of simmering water using dessertspoon. Poach about 2 minutes on each side. Do not allow water to boil or quenelles will fall apart. Drain quenelles on absorbent paper, serve with tomato onion sauce.

Tomato Onion Sauce: Heat oil in pan, add garlic and onion, cook, stirring, until onion is soft. Add paste, undrained crushed tomatoes and sugar, simmer, covered, 5 minutes. Blend or process mixture until well combined; strain.

Serves 4.

- Quenelle mixture can be made a day ahead. Poach quenelles just before serving. Sauce can be made a day ahead.
- Storage: Quenelle mixture and sauce, covered, in refrigerator.
- Freeze: Not suitable.
- Microwave: Not suitable.

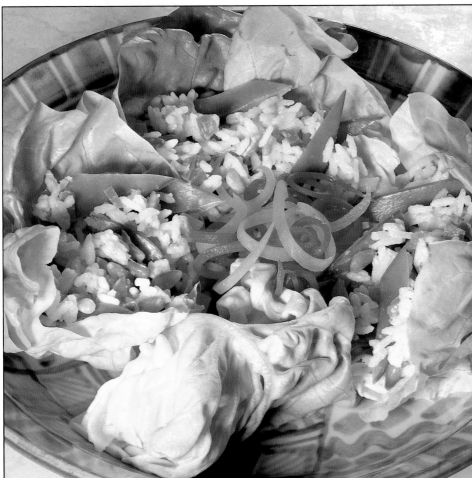

ABOVE LEFT: From top: Pasta with Creamy Basil and Almond Sauce; Creamy Pasta with Spinach and Bacon.
RIGHT: Coconut Rice in Lettuce Rolls.
ABOVE RIGHT: Ricotta, Chicken and Spinach Quenelles.

MUSHROOM, BACON AND PORT WINE TIMBALES

2 tablespoons (¼ stick) butter
1lb small button mushrooms, sliced
3 slices bacon, chopped
4 teaspoons all-purpose flour
3 tablespoons port wine
¾ cup heavy cream
3 eggs, lightly beaten

TOMATO SAUCE
⅓ cup tomato puree
⅓ cup sour cream
¼ cup French dressing
½ teaspoon Worcestershire sauce
¼ teaspoon sugar

Melt butter in skillet, add mushrooms and bacon, cook, stirring, until mushrooms are tender. Stir in flour, cook, stirring, 1 minute. Remove from heat, gradually stir in wine and cream, stir over high heat until mixture boils and thickens.

Transfer mixture to bowl, stand 5 minutes; quickly stir in eggs. Pour mixture evenly into 6 greased timbale molds (½ cup capacity). Cover each mold with greased foil, place in roasting pan, pour in enough boiling water to come halfway up sides of molds.

Bake in 350°F oven about 45 minutes or until timbales are just set. Stand 5 minutes before turning onto plates; serve with tomato sauce.

Tomato Sauce: Combine all ingredients in small bowl.

Serves 6.

- Timbales best made just before serving. Sauce can be made several hours ahead.
- Storage: Covered, in refrigerator.
- Freeze: Not suitable.
- Microwave: Timbale mixture suitable.

SWEET POTATO TRIANGLES WITH SPICY DIPPING SAUCE

¾lb sweet potato, chopped
4 green onions, chopped
¼ teaspoon ground cumin
7oz ricotta cheese
3 tablespoons grated Parmesan cheese
5 sheets phyllo pastry
3oz (¾ stick) butter, melted

SPICY DIPPING SAUCE
1 teaspoon cornstarch
½ cup water
4 teaspoons rice vinegar
4 teaspoons dark brown sugar
½ teaspoon sambal oelek
½ teaspoon grated fresh gingerroot

Boil, steam or microwave potato until tender; drain. Blend or process potato until smooth, add onions, cumin and cheeses, process until combined; cool.

Brush 1 sheet of pastry with butter, cut evenly into 3 strips about 3½ inches wide. Place 1 rounded tablespoon of mixture on 1 end of each strip. Take corner of pastry and fold over filling to form a triangle as shown.

Continue folding over to end of pastry strip. Repeat folding with remaining pastry and filling.

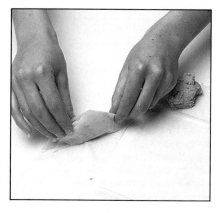

Place triangles in single layer onto lightly greased baking sheet, brush with remaining butter. Just before serving, bake in 375°F oven about 20 minutes or until golden brown. Serve with spicy dipping sauce.

Spicy Dipping Sauce: Blend cornstarch and water in pan, add remaining ingredients, stir over high heat until mixture boils and thickens slightly.

Makes 15.

- Triangles can be prepared a day ahead. Sauce can be made a day ahead.
- Storage: Covered, in refrigerator.
- Freeze: Not suitable.
- Microwave: Potato and sauce suitable.

BRAISED FENNEL AND ONION

1 fennel bulb
¼ cup (½ stick) butter
1 onion, sliced
1 clove garlic, minced
1 teaspoon grated lemon zest
½ large chicken bouillon cube
1 teaspoon cornstarch
¾ cup water
3 tablespoons grated Parmesan cheese

Chop some of the fennel leaves finely to give 4 teaspoons chopped leaves; slice fennel bulb. Heat butter in skillet, add fennel, cook, stirring, 2 minutes. Add onion and garlic, cook, stirring, until onion is soft. Add zest, crumbled bouillon cube and blended cornstarch and water, stir over high heat until mixture boils and thickens; stir in fennel leaves. Serve with cheese.

Serves 4.

- Recipe best made just before serving.
- Freeze: Not suitable.
- Microwave: Suitable.

RIGHT: From top: Sweet Potato Triangles with Spicy Dipping Sauce; Braised Fennel and Onion.
ABOVE LEFT: Mushroom, Bacon and Port Wine Timbales.

ASPARAGUS RICE MOLDS WITH TWO SAUCES

3 cups water
1 small chicken bouillon cube
½ cup long-grain rice
8 fresh asparagus spears
4 teaspoons chopped fresh parsley
2 cherry tomatoes, halved

TOMATO SAUCE
1 tablespoon butter
2 very ripe tomatoes,
    roughly chopped
¼ teaspoon sugar
½ teaspoon tomato paste
½ cup water

CREAM SAUCE
¾ cup heavy cream
4 teaspoons dry white wine
4 teaspoons fresh lemon juice

Combine water and crumbled bouillon cube in pan, bring to boil, add rice, boil, uncovered, until tender; drain. Boil, steam or microwave asparagus until just tender, remove tips and set aside. Chop stalks finely, combine with rice and parsley in bowl. Place a cherry tomato half, rounded-side-down, in base of each of 4 molds (½ cup capacity). Spoon rice mixture evenly into molds, press down firmly with back of spoon. Unmold onto plates, spoon each sauce around molds; top with asparagus tips.
Tomato Sauce: Melt butter in pan, add remaining ingredients, simmer, covered, 15 minutes; strain.
Cream Sauce: Combine cream, wine and juice in small bowl; mix well.

Serves 4.

■ Recipe can be made a day ahead.
■ Storage: Covered, in refrigerator.
■ Freeze: Not suitable.
■ Microwave: Suitable.

MUSHROOM CREPES WITH CREAMY CHIVE SAUCE

¼ cup (½ stick) butter
½lb button mushrooms, halved
5oz oyster mushrooms

CREPES
¼ cup all-purpose flour
1 egg
2 teaspoons light olive oil
½ cup milk

CREAMY CHIVE SAUCE
1 teaspoon butter
1½ teaspoons all-purpose flour
3 tablespoons dry white wine
4 teaspoons chopped fresh chives
½ cup heavy cream
3 tablespoons milk
3 tablespoons sour cream
4 teaspoons chopped fresh
    chives, extra

Melt butter in skillet, add button mushrooms, cook, stirring, 1 minute. Stir in oyster mushrooms, cook, stirring, about 1 minute or until just tender.

Heat crepes gently on plate over simmering water or in 350°F oven (covered with foil) about 5 minutes. Divide mushroom mixture evenly over crepes, fold into quarters; serve with chive sauce.
Crepes: Sift flour into bowl, gradually stir in combined egg, oil and milk, mix to a smooth batter (or blend or process all ingredients until smooth). Cover, stand 30 minutes. Pour 3 to 4 tablespoons batter into heated greased crepe pan, cook until lightly browned underneath. Turn crepe, brown on other side. Repeat with remaining batter. You will need 6 crepes.
Creamy Chive Sauce: Blend butter and flour in cup with spoon. Combine wine, chives, cream and milk in pan, bring to boil, stir in blended butter and flour. Stir over heat until sauce boils and thickens. Remove from heat, blend or process until smooth, strain, stir in sour cream and extra chives. Reheat creamy chive sauce gently before serving.

Serves 6.

■ Assemble crepes just before serving. Unfilled crepes can be made up to 2 days ahead. Sauce best made just before serving.
■ Storage: Crepes, layered with paper, in refrigerator.
■ Freeze: Unfilled crepes suitable.
■ Microwave: Sauce suitable.

ABOVE: Mushroom Crepes with Creamy Chive Sauce.
LEFT: Asparagus Rice Molds with Two Sauces.

RATATOUILLE MOLDS WITH WHITE WINE SAUCE

½lb eggplant, chopped
coarse (kosher) salt
3 tablespoons olive oil
1 small onion, finely chopped
1 clove garlic, minced
10oz zucchini, thinly sliced
1 green bell pepper, chopped
1 large tomato, peeled, chopped
3 tablespoons tomato paste
¼ teaspoon cracked black
    peppercorns

WHITE WINE SAUCE
½ cup dry white wine
2 tablespoons (¼ stick) butter
4 teaspoons all-purpose flour
1 large vegetable bouillon cube
1 cup water
¼ cup heavy cream

Place eggplant on wire rack, sprinkle with salt, stand 20 minutes. Rinse under cold water, pat dry with absorbent paper. Heat oil in skillet, add onion and garlic, cook, stirring, until onion is soft. Add eggplant, zucchini and pepper, cook, stirring, until eggplant is soft; stir in remaining ingredients. Cover, simmer about 20 minutes or until most liquid is evaporated, stirring occasionally; cool slightly.

Lightly grease 4 molds (½ cup capacity). Place strips of greased foil down sides and across bases of molds. Spoon ratatouille mixture into molds, cover, refrigerate several hours. Turn onto plates, serve with white wine sauce.

White Wine Sauce: Place wine in pan, simmer, uncovered, until wine is reduced to about 3 tablespoons. Melt butter in pan, stir in flour, cook, stirring, 1 minute. Remove from heat, gradually stir in combined crumbled bouillon cube, water and wine, stir over high heat until mixture boils and thickens; stir in cream.

Serves 4.

■ Molds can be made a day ahead.
■ Storage: Covered, in refrigerator.
■ Freeze: Not suitable.
■ Microwave: Sauce suitable.

TOMATO SOUFFLES

½ cup packaged unseasoned
    bread crumbs
3 tablespoons butter
1 small onion, finely chopped
3 tablespoons all-purpose flour
1 cup milk
3 tablespoons tomato paste
4 teaspoons finely chopped
    fresh basil
3 eggs, separated

Grease 4 souffle dishes (½ cup capacity), sprinkle with bread crumbs. Melt butter in pan, add onion, cook, stirring, until onion is soft. Stir in flour, cook, stirring, 1 minute. Remove from heat, gradually stir in milk, stir over high heat until mixture boils and thickens. Transfer to bowl, stir in tomato paste and basil, cover; stand 5 minutes.

Stir in egg yolks. Beat egg whites in small bowl with electric mixer until soft peaks form, fold into onion mixture in 2 batches. Place dishes onto baking sheet, pour mixture evenly into dishes. Bake in 375˚F oven about 20 minutes or until puffed and lightly browned.

Serves 4.

■ Make souffles just before serving.
■ Freeze: Not suitable.
■ Microwave: Souffle mixture suitable.

LEFT: Ratatouille Molds with White Wine Sauce.
RIGHT: Tomato Souffles.

Terrines & Pates

Most terrines and pates can be made in advance, saving time before a dinner party or lunch. The ideal accompaniments for both are salad vegetables, bread or crackers. Pates are served as a spread and mostly have a velvety texture. Terrines are more substantial and will cut beautifully, as required. We have not recommended freezing terrines because we prefer the texture with out freezing.

CHICKEN, HAM AND APRICOT TERRINES

2 cups (½lb) dried apricots, chopped
½lb ham, chopped
bay leaves
1lb boneless, skinless chicken breast halves, chopped
¾lb chicken thighs, boned, skinned, chopped
1 onion, chopped
2 cloves garlic, minced
½ cup heavy cream
3 tablespoons brandy
1 egg
1 stalk celery, chopped

LEMON MAYONNAISE
½ cup mayonnaise
4 teaspoons fresh parsley, chopped
1 teaspoon grated lemon zest
3 tablespoons fresh lemon juice
¼ teaspoon sugar

Decorate bases of 2 greased 3 inch x 10 inch baking pans with some of the apricots, ham and bay leaves.

Blend or process all chicken, onion, garlic, cream, brandy and egg until well combined. Transfer mixture to large bowl, stir in ham, celery and apricots, spread evenly into prepared pans; press down firmly. Cover pans with foil, place into roasting pan, pour in enough boiling water to come halfway up sides of pans, bake in 350°F oven 1½ hours. Remove from oven, drain away excess juices, place weights on top of foil, cool to room temperature; refrigerate overnight. Turn terrines out, serve terrines sliced with lemon mayonnaise.

Lemon Mayonnaise: Combine all ingredients in small bowl.

- Terrines can be made 3 days ahead.
- Storage: Covered, in refrigerator.
- Freeze: Not suitable.
- Microwave: Not suitable.

RIGHT: From top: Chicken, Ham and Apricot Terrine; Pork and Veal Terrine with Cranberry Port Wine Sauce.

PORK AND VEAL TERRINE WITH CRANBERRY PORT WINE SAUCE

1 tablespoon butter
1 onion, chopped
1 clove garlic, minced
3 green onions, chopped
½lb chicken livers
4 teaspoons brandy
1lb ground pork and veal
2 teaspoons grated orange zest
4 teaspoons Cointreau
2 eggs, lightly beaten
4 teaspoons olive oil
½lb pork tenderloin
7 thick slices bacon

CRANBERRY PORT WINE SAUCE
½ cup port wine
½ cup cranberry sauce
4 teaspoons grated orange zest
¼ cup fresh orange juice
1 teaspoon grated lemon zest
2 teaspoons fresh lemon juice
1 teaspoon fresh thyme,
  finely chopped

Heat butter in large skillet, add onion, garlic and green onions, cook, stirring, until onion is soft. Add livers, cook, stirring, about 3 minutes or until changed in color. Stir in brandy; cool. Blend or process mixture until smooth, transfer mixture to large bowl. Stir in ground pork and veal, zest, liqueur and eggs.

Heat oil in skillet, add pork tenderloin, cook over hight heat until well browned all over; drain on absorbent paper.

Line ovenproof loaf dish (5 cup capacity) with bacon, spoon half the pork and veal mixture into dish, top with pork tenderloin. Fold ends of bacon over filling, cover dish tightly with foil.

Place terrine in roasting pan, pour in enough boiling water to come halfway up sides of dish. Bake in 300˚F oven 2 hours, stand 10 minutes; cool, refrigerate overnight. Serve sliced terrine with cranberry port wine sauce.

Cranberry Port Wine Sauce: Combine all ingredients in pan, simmer, uncovered, about 10 minutes or until mixture reduces by half. Cool before serving.

- Terrine and sauce can be made 3 days ahead.
- Storage: Covered, in refrigerator.
- Freeze: Not suitable.
- Microwave: Not suitable.

LOBSTER AND GREEN PEPPERCORN PATE

1 cooked lobster tail
1 teaspoon unflavored gelatin
3 tablespoons water
4 teaspoons dry white wine
4 teaspoons fresh lemon juice
1 lemon
parsley
1/4 cup fresh lemon juice, extra
4 teaspoons brandy
4 teaspoons dry white wine
2 teaspoons creamed horseradish
2 teaspoons unflavored gelatin, extra
4 teaspoons water, extra
4 teaspoons green peppercorns
1 1/4 cups whipping cream
1 egg white

WHITE WINE SAUCE
1/4 cup (1/2 stick) butter
1 small onion, chopped
2 cloves garlic, minced
1 small carrot, chopped
1 small stalk celery, chopped
1 cup dry white wine
2 tomatoes, chopped
1 tablespoon tomato paste
1 small chicken bouillon cube
2/3 cup water
1/2 cup heavy cream

Remove lobster meat from shell in 1 piece, chop 4 x 1/2 inch pink pieces for garnish, chop remaining lobster. Wash shell, reserve for sauce. Rinse 4 molds (1/2 cup capacity) with water. Sprinkle gelatin over water in cup, stand in small pan of simmering water, stir until dissolved. Stir in wine and juice.

Pour a little gelatin mixture into each mold until base is just covered; refrigerate until set. Arrange some lemon zest, reserved lobster pieces and parsley over jelly; carefully pour some more gelatin mixture over garnish; refrigerate until set.

Process lobster, extra juice, brandy, wine and horseradish until smooth, transfer to bowl. Sprinkle extra gelatin over extra water in cup, stand in small pan of simmering water, stir until dissolved. Cool 5 minutes, stir into lobster mixture with peppercorns. Beat cream until firm peaks form, fold into lobster mixture. Beat egg white until firm peaks form, fold into lobster mixture. Divide mixture evenly between molds; cover, refrigerate several hours or overnight. Turn onto plates, serve with warm white wine sauce.

White Wine Sauce: Melt butter in pan, add onion, garlic, carrot and celery, cook, stirring, 3 minutes. Crush lobster shell, add to pan with wine, tomatoes, paste, crumbled bouillon cube and water. Simmer, uncovered, about 10 minutes or until reduced by one-third. Strain mixture, return to clean pan, add cream, simmer, uncovered, about 10 minutes or until reduced by half.

- Pate can be made 2 days ahead.
- Storage: Covered, in refrigerator.
- Freeze: Not suitable.
- Microwave: Gelatin suitable.

SALMON AND FISH TERRINE WITH CAPER MAYONNAISE

10 large spinach leaves

SALMON MOUSSE
10oz Atlantic salmon
3 1/2 oz white fish fillet
1/4 lb uncooked shrimp, shelled
1 egg white
1 cup heavy cream
1 teaspoon grated lemon zest
2 teaspoons fresh lemon juice
1/2 teaspoon paprika

FISH MOUSSE
14oz white fish fillets
1/4 lb uncooked shrimp, shelled
1 egg white
1 cup heavy cream
2 teaspoons brandy
3 tablespoons chopped fresh chives

CAPER MAYONNAISE
1/3 cup mayonnaise
4 teaspoons drained capers, chopped
1/2 teaspoon paprika
1/4 teaspoon grated lemon zest
2 teaspoons fresh lemon juice
2 teaspoons water

Line base and sides of 4 inch x 8 inch ovenproof loaf dish with plastic wrap. Boil, just steam or microwave spinach leaves until wilted, rinse under cold water; drain well. Lay spinach leaves out in single layer on sheet of plastic wrap in a 6 inch x 10 inch rectangle.

Spread spinach evenly with 1/2 cup of the salmon mousse.

Roll up from side like a jelly-roll, using the plastic to lift and guide mixture. Roll securely in foil, twist ends firmly to hold in shape. Poach roll in pan of simmering water 10 minutes; cool to room temperature. Remove foil.

Spread fish mousse into prepared dish in triangular shape, as shown.

Form a slight hollow in center of mousse and insert spinach roll, trim ends, if necessary; press in gently.

Spread with the remaining salmon mousse, cover with plastic wrap.

Cover dish with foil, place in roasting pan, pour in enough boiling water to come halfway up sides of loaf dish. Bake in 350°F oven about 1 1/2 hours or until firm to touch; cool, refrigerate overnight. Serve sliced terrine with caper mayonnaise.

Salmon Mousse: Process both fish, shrimp and egg white until smooth. Add cream, zest, juice and paprika, process until just combined; transfer to bowl, cover, refrigerate about 15 minutes or until just firm.

Fish Mousse: Process fish, shrimp and egg white until smooth. Add cream, brandy and chives, process until just combined. Transfer to bowl, cover, refrigerate until firm.

Caper Mayonnaise: Combine all ingredients in bowl.

- Terrine can be made 2 days ahead.
- Storage: Covered, in refrigerator.
- Freeze: Not suitable.
- Microwave: Not suitable.

RIGHT: From top: Salmon and Fish Terrine with Caper Mayonnaise; Lobster and Green Peppercorn Pate.

GRAND MARNIER VELVET PATE

Ask your butcher to save you some
bone marrow for this recipe.

¾lb chicken livers
3 tablespoons Grand Marnier
1 tablespoon butter
1 slice bacon, finely chopped
1 clove garlic, minced
⅓ cup fresh orange juice
½ small chicken bouillon cube
1 cup fresh bread crumbs
3 tablespoons chopped fresh parsley
2oz bone marrow
2 eggs
⅓ cup heavy cream
½ cup (1 stick) butter, melted, extra

Place livers in bowl with liqueur, stand
2 hours. Drain livers, reserve liqueur. Heat
butter in skillet, add bacon and garlic,
cook, stirring, until bacon is crisp. Add
juice, crumbled bouillon cube and bread
crumbs, stir over heat until combined.
Blend or process bacon mixture, livers,
parsley, bone marrow, eggs, cream and
reserved liqueur until smooth. Push mixture through sieve.

Pour into 4 ovenproof dishes (1½ cup
capacity), cover each dish with lightly
greased foil. Place dishes in roasting pan,
pour in enough boiling water to come
halfway up sides of dishes. Bake in 325°F
oven about 30 minutes or until set.
Remove dishes; cool. Pour extra butter
over each pate. Refrigerate overnight.

■ Pate can be made 3 days ahead.
■ Storage: Covered, in refrigerator.
■ Freeze: Not suitable.
■ Microwave: Not suitable.

RIGHT: Grand Marnier Velvet Pate.

WARM VEGETABLE TERRINE WITH MUSHROOM SAUCE

½ cup (1 stick) butter
½ cup all-purpose flour
1½ cups milk
½ cup grated cheddar cheese
8 eggs, lightly beaten
10oz broccoli, chopped
4 carrots
14oz cauliflower, chopped

FRESH MUSHROOM SAUCE
¼ cup (½ stick) butter
7oz button mushrooms, sliced
1¼ cups heavy cream

Melt butter in pan, add flour, cook, stirring, 2 minutes. Remove from heat, gradually stir in milk, stir over high heat until mixture boils and thickens. Remove from heat, add cheese, stir until melted; cool 10 minutes. Stir in eggs, divide mixture evenly into 3 portions. Boil, steam or microwave vegetables until tender.

Line 5½ inch x 8 inch loaf pan with plastic wrap. Blend or process broccoli with one-third of the sauce until smooth. Spread broccoli mixture into prepared pan. Repeat this process with carrots, cauliflower and the remaining sauce. Cover pan with greased foil, place pan into roasting pan, pour in enough boiling water to come halfway up sides of pan. Bake in 350°F oven about 2¼ hours or until firm; stand 15 minutes before turning out. Serve sliced terrine with fresh mushroom sauce.

Fresh Mushroom Sauce: Melt butter in pan, add mushrooms, cook, stirring, 2 minutes. Add cream, simmer, uncovered, about 10 minutes or until the mushroom mixture is slightly thickened.

■ Terrine can be prepared 2 days ahead. Sauce can be prepared a day ahead.
■ Storage: Covered, in refrigerator.
■ Freeze: Not suitable.
■ Microwave: Sauce suitable.

RIGHT: From left: Smoked Fish and Gingerroot Pate, Seafood Terrine with Scallop Sauce.
BELOW: Warm Vegetable Terrine with Mushroom Sauce.

SMOKED FISH AND GINGERROOT PATE

2lb smoked fish fillets
1 cup (2 sticks) unsalted butter, softened
1 teaspoon grated fresh gingerroot
⅛ teaspoon cayenne pepper
3 tablespoons heavy cream

Line 3 inch x 10 inch baking pan with foil. Poach or microwave fish until cooked; drain; cool.

Blend or process fish, butter, gingerroot, pepper and cream until well combined. Press mixture firmly into prepared pan, smooth top. Cover, refrigerate overnight or until firm. Turn pate out, cut into slices to serve.

■ Pate can be made 3 days ahead.
■ Storage: Covered, in refrigerator.
■ Freeze: Not suitable.
■ Microwave: Suitable.

SEAFOOD TERRINE WITH SCALLOP SAUCE

15oz sliced smoked salmon

SEAFOOD FILLING
1lb sea scallops
¾lb trout fillet
10oz sour cream
⅓ cup fresh lemon juice
4 teaspoons horseradish cream

2 teaspoons paprika
2 teaspoons unflavored gelatin
4 teaspoons water
2 egg whites

FISH FILLING
10oz trout fillet
1 teaspoon chopped fresh dill

SCALLOP SAUCE
¼ cup water
4 teaspoons dry white wine
4 teaspoons fresh lemon juice
1¼ cups heavy cream
¼ cup mayonnaise
3 tablespoons chopped fresh dill

Rinse ovenproof dish (5 cup capacity) with cold water, line with plastic wrap. Line dish with two-thirds of the smoked salmon, slightly overlapping each slice and allowing ends to overhang. Spread half the seafood filling into dish, cover with fish filling, then remaining seafood filling.

Fold in smoked salmon ends over seafood filling, use remaining salmon to cover top of terrine. Cover, refrigerate several hours or overnight. Turn terrine out, remove plastic wrap. Slice terrine, serve with sauce and lime, if desired.

Seafood Filling: Remove coral from half the scallops for sauce; reserve another 4 whole scallops for sauce. Wrap fish and remaining scallops in lightly greased foil, place in ovenproof dish, bake in 350°F

oven about 20 minutes or until seafood is cooked. Blend or process fish and scallop mixture with sour cream, juice, horseradish and paprika until smooth; transfer to large bowl.

Sprinkle gelatin over water in cup, stand in small pan of simmering water, stir until dissolved, stir into seafood mixture. Beat egg whites in small bowl until soft peaks form, fold into seafood mixture.

Fish Filling: Wrap fish in lightly greased foil, place in ovenproof dish, bake in 350°F oven about 10 minutes or until fish is cooked, cool, flake with fork, combine in bowl with dill.

Scallop Sauce: Combine water, wine, juice, reserved scallop coral and the 4 reserved scallops in pan. Simmer gently over heat, without boiling, about 2 minutes or until scallops are cooked, drain; cool. Blend or process scallop mixture with cream and mayonnaise until well combined. Stir in dill.

■ Terrine can be made a day ahead.
■ Storage: Covered, in refrigerator.
■ Freeze: Not suitable.
■ Microwave: Gelatin suitable.

DEER LIVER TERRINE WITH BLACKBERRY SAUCE

1lb deer liver
milk
1 teaspoon grated lemon zest
1 teaspoon grated orange zest
1 onion, chopped
2 juniper berries, crushed
¼ teaspoon dried thyme leaves
¼ teaspoon dried marjoram leaves
¼ teaspoon dried basil leaves
1 bay leaf
¼ cup brandy
¼ cup port wine
2 eggs
1 cup fresh white bread crumbs
½ cup shelled pistachio nuts
20 thin slices bacon

BROWN SAUCE
1 tablespoon butter
4 teaspoons all-purpose flour
½ cup water
½ large beef bouillon cube

BLACKBERRY SAUCE
½lb blackberries
¼ cup sugar
½ teaspoon grated orange zest
4 teaspoons fresh orange juice
2 teaspoons fresh lemon juice
3 tablespoons water
4 teaspoons Cassis

Remove the thin layer of skin and membrane from liver. Cut liver into large pieces, place in bowl, cover with milk, refrigerate overnight.

Drain liver and wash under cold water; drain. Return liver to bowl, add zests, onion, berries, herbs, bay leaf, brandy and port wine, cover; refrigerate 3 hours. Discard bay leaf, process mixture until smooth. Add eggs, process until combined. Return mixture to large bowl, stir in bread crumbs, nuts and brown sauce.

Remove rind from bacon, overlap slices on sheet of baking paper in a 7 inch x 10 inch rectangle. Spread half the liver mixture onto long side of bacon rectangle. Roll up like a jelly-roll, using the paper to lift and guide the roll. Discard paper. Wrap roll securely in foil, twist ends tightly. Repeat with remaining mixture.

Poach rolls in large shallow pan of simmering water 25 minutes, cool; refrigerate several hours or overnight. Serve sliced terrine with blackberry sauce.

Brown Sauce: Melt butter in pan, add flour, cook, stirring, until golden brown. Remove from heat, gradually stir in water and crumbled bouillon cube. Stir over high heat until mixture boils; cool.

Blackberry Sauce: Combine blackberries, sugar, zest, juices and water in pan, simmer 1 minute. Strain, add liqueur; cool.

■ Terrine can be made 2 days ahead.
■ Storage: Covered, in refrigerator.
■ Freeze: Not suitable.
■ Microwave: Sauces suitable.

HERBED LAMB TERRINE EN CROUTE

2 tablespoons (¼ stick) butter
1 clove garlic, minced
1 onion chopped
¼lb chicken livers, chopped
3 tablespoons port wine
¼ cup heavy cream
2lb lamb chops
½lb ground pork and veal
1 egg
3 tablespoons chopped
    fresh rosemary
3 tablespoons chopped fresh mint
3 tablespoons chopped fresh parsley
3 tablespoons chopped fresh basil
4 teaspoons grated lemon zest
1 egg, lightly beaten, extra

PASTRY
1½ cups all-purpose flour
¾ cup self-rising flour
5oz (1¼ sticks) butter, chopped
3 tablespoons fresh lemon juice
3 tablespoons water, approximately

Melt butter in skillet, add garlic and onion, cook, stirring, until onion is soft. Add livers, cook, stirring, until changed in color. Stir in wine and cream; cool 5 minutes.

Remove lamb from bones, blend or process half the lamb until finely ground. Add chicken liver mixture, ground pork and veal, egg, herbs and zest; blend or process until combined. Transfer mixture to large bowl, chop remaining lamb, add to mixture. Spread into greased 5½ inch

x 8 inch loaf pan, cover with foil. Stand pan in roasting pan, pour in enough boiling water to come halfway up sides of loaf pan, bake in 350°F oven 1½ hours. Stand 5 minutes, turn onto wire rack; drain 15 minutes. Return to pan, cover with foil, place a weight on top; refrigerate overnight.

Roll pastry to 14 inch x 18 inch rectangle; trim edges. Place terrine in center of pastry, cut out corners.

Brush edges with extra egg, wrap terrine in pastry, press edges together firmly. Turn terrine over, place onto lightly greased baking sheet. Decorate with shapes cut from remaining pastry, brush pastry all over with extra egg. Bake in 375°F oven 15 minutes, reduce heat to 350°F, bake further 20 minutes. Cool to room temperature, refrigerate several hours or overnight before cutting.

Pastry: Sift flours into bowl, rub in butter. Add juice and enough water to mix to a firm dough (or pastry can be made in processor). Knead gently on lightly floured surface 20 minutes before using.

■ Terrine (without pastry) can be made 3 days ahead.
■ Storage: Covered, in refrigerator.
■ Freeze: Not suitable.
■ Microwave: Not suitable.

ABOVE: From left: Deer Liver Terrine with Blackberry Sauce; Herbed Lamb Terrine en Croute.

Appetizers

Seafood

A seafood appetizer teams well with any main course, even more seafood of another type. Buy seafood in season because it will be cheapest, have the best flavor and is unlikely to be frozen. Seafood is usually at its best cooked and served at once to maintain good texture and flavor.

SEAFOOD RATATOUILLE TARTS

PASTRY
2 cups all-purpose flour
5oz (1¼ sticks) butter
1 egg yolk
1 teaspoon fresh lemon juice
4 teaspoons water, approximately

SEAFOOD RATATOUILLE
¾lb uncooked shrimp, shelled
5oz sea scallops
5oz cleaned squid
4 teaspoons olive oil
1 clove garlic, minced
4 teaspoons olive oil, extra
1 onion, chopped
2 small zucchini, chopped
2 tomatoes, peeled, seeded, chopped
¼ teaspoon dried oregano leaves
⅓ cup dry white wine
4 teaspoons tomato paste

Pastry: Sift flour into bowl, rub in butter. Add egg yolk, juice and enough water to mix to firm dough. Turn pastry onto lightly floured surface, knead lightly until smooth. Divide pastry into 6 portions, cover, refrigerate 30 minutes.

Roll portions between plastic wrap until large enough to line 6 x 4 inch flan pans, trim edges. Cover each pastry case with baking paper, fill with dried beans or rice, bake in 375°F oven 7 minutes. Remove beans and paper. Bake pastry cases further 7 minutes or until lightly browned. Stand 10 minutes before removing from pans. Serve filled with ratatouille.

Seafood Ratatouille: Cut shrimp and scallops in half, cut cleaned squid open, cut squid into bite-sized pieces.

Heat oil in skillet, add garlic and seafood, stir-fry about 3 minutes or until seafood is cooked; remove from skillet. Heat extra oil in skillet, add onion, cook, stirring, until soft. Stir in zucchini, tomatoes, oregano, wine and tomato paste. Simmer, uncovered, about 3 minutes or until slightly thickened. Add seafood, reheat gently.

Makes 6.

- Unfilled pastry cases can made a week ahead. Ratatouille can be made 2 days ahead, add seafood before serving.
- Storage: Pastry cases, in airtight container. Ratatouille, covered, in refrigerator.
- Freeze: Pastry cases suitable.
- Microwave: Not suitable.

BUTTERFLIED BASIL SHRIMP

1lb uncooked jumbo shrimp

BASIL BUTTER
3oz (¾ stick) butter
2 teaspoons chopped fresh basil
2 green onions, finely chopped
2 small fresh red chili peppers, finely chopped
1 clove garlic, minced

Shell shrimp, leaving tails intact; remove back veins. Cut shrimp along back, but not right through; flatten shrimp gently with blade of large knife or with hand.

Brush shrimp with basil butter, place cut-side-down on broiler tray, broil until just cooked, brushing occasionally with basil butter.

Basil Butter: Melt butter in pan, stir in basil, onions, chili peppers and garlic.

Serves 4.

- Basil butter can be made a week ahead.
- Storage: Covered, in refrigerator.
- Freeze: Butter suitable.
- Microwave: Suitable.

LEFT: From top: Butterflied Basil Shrimp; Seafood Ratatouille Tarts.

LAYERED SALMON CREPES WITH SPINACH MAYONNAISE

CREPES
½ cup all-purpose flour
2 eggs, lightly beaten
½ cup milk
2 teaspoons light olive oil

SALMON FILLING
8oz package cream cheese
3 tablespoons fresh lemon juice
4 teaspoons mayonnaise
15oz can red salmon, drained
3 tablespoons chopped fresh parsley
1 small onion, finely chopped

SPINACH MAYONNAISE
½ bunch (10oz) spinach
2 egg yolks
3 tablespoons fresh lemon juice
1 cup light olive oil
1 teaspoon French mustard
3 tablespoons hot water

Sift flour into bowl, gradually stir in combined eggs, milk and oil, mix to a smooth batter (or blend or process all ingredients until smooth). Cover, stand 30 minutes. Pour 3 to 4 tablespoons of batter into 8 inch heated greased crepe pan; cook until crepe is lightly browned underneath. Turn crepe, brown on other side. Repeat with remaining batter. You will need 4 crepes.

Grease shallow 8 inch baking pan, line with baking paper. Cut crepes to fit inside the pan if necessary. Place a crepe into pan, spread one-third of salmon filling over crepe, top with another crepe. Continue layering crepes and salmon filling, finishing with a crepe; cover, refrigerate overnight. Serve with spinach mayonnaise.

Salmon Filling: Beat cream cheese in bowl with electric mixer until smooth, add juice, mayonnaise and salmon, beat until smooth. Stir in parsley and onion.

Spinach Mayonnaise: Boil, steam or microwave spinach until tender, drain, rinse under cold water; drain well on absorbent paper. Blend or process egg yolks and juice, gradually add oil in thin stream while motor is operating. Add spinach, mustard and water, blend until smooth.

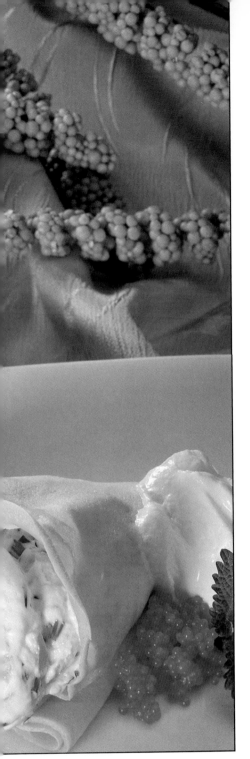

SMOKED SALMON CONES WITH SOUR CREAM AND CAVIAR

¾ cup all-purpose flour
3 eggs, lightly beaten
1 cup milk
4 teaspoons light olive oil
⅓ cup sour cream
1½oz red lumpfish caviar
SMOKED SALMON FILLING
4oz package cream cheese, softened
3 tablespoons sour cream
2 teaspoons fresh lemon juice
2 teaspoons chopped fresh dill
4 teaspoons chopped fresh chives
1 teaspoon chopped fresh mint
1½oz smoked salmon, finely chopped

Sift flour into bowl, gradually stir in combined eggs, milk and oil, mix to a smooth batter (or blend or process all ingredients until smooth). Cover, stand 30 minutes. Pour 3 to 4 tablespoons of batter into heated greased crepe pan; cook until lightly browned underneath. Turn crepe, brown on other side. Repeat with remaining batter. You will need 8 crepes.

Fold each crepe in half, then half again to form a cone shape.

Fit piping bag with ½ inch plain tube, fill with salmon filling, pipe mixture into crepe cones, serve with sour cream and caviar.
Smoked Salmon Filling: Beat cream cheese in bowl until smooth, stir in remaining ingredients.

Serves 4.

- Crepes and filling can be made separately a day ahead.
- Storage: Filling, covered, in refrigerator. Unfilled crepes, layered with paper, in refrigerator.
- Freeze: Unfilled crepes suitable.
- Microwave: Not suitable.

Serves 6 to 8.

- Recipe can be made 2 days ahead. Unfilled crepes can be made 2 days ahead.
- Storage: Covered, in refrigerator. Unfilled crepes, layered with paper, in refrigerator.
- Freeze: Unfilled crepes suitable.
- Microwave: Not suitable.

MARINATED SEAFOOD

The seafood is uncooked but the action of the citrus juice "cooks" the seafood, making it opaque; it appears and tastes cooked.

½lb white fish fillets
¼lb uncooked shrimp, shelled
¼lb sea scallops
¾ cup fresh lemon juice
½ cup fresh lime juice
¼ cup olive oil
4 teaspoons white wine vinegar
1 clove garlic, minced
¼ teaspoon dried oregano leaves
1 onion, sliced
1 tomato, peeled, seeded, chopped
1 tablespoon canned drained jalapeno chili peppers, chopped
1oz stuffed green olives, sliced
1 red leaf lettuce

Cut fish into fine strips, combine in bowl with shrimp, scallops and juices; cover, refrigerate overnight.

Next day, drain seafood, reserve ½ cup marinade. Combine reserved marinade with oil, vinegar, garlic and oregano in bowl, add onion, tomato, chili peppers, olives and seafood. Cover, refrigerate further 2 hours before serving on lettuce leaves.

Serves 4.

- Recipe best made a day ahead.
- Storage: Covered, in refrigerator.
- Freeze: Not suitable.

BELOW: Marinated Seafood.
LEFT: From top: Layered Salmon Crepes with Spinach Mayonnaise; Smoked Salmon Cones with Sour Cream and Caviar.

SCALLOP MOUSSELINE WITH SAFFRON SAUCE

1 tablespoon butter
4 teaspoons all-purpose flour
½ cup milk
3 tablespoons heavy cream
5oz sea scallops
2 eggs
4 teaspoons chopped fresh dill
1 cup water
¼ cup fresh lemon juice
12 shucked oysters

SAFFRON SAUCE
1 tablespoon butter
1 onion, chopped
⅔ cup water
⅓ cup dry white wine
½ small chicken bouillon cube
tiny pinch ground saffron
½ cup heavy cream
4 teaspoons cornstarch
4 teaspoons water, extra

Grease 6 small savarin molds (¼ cup capacity). Melt butter in pan, add flour, cook, stirring, 1 minute. Remove from heat, gradually stir in milk and cream, stir over high heat until mixture boils and thickens. Remove mixture from heat, cover; stand 5 minutes.

Blend or process scallops until smooth, add milk mixture and eggs, process until combined, stir in dill.

Pour into prepared molds, cover with greased foil, place in roasting pan, pour in enough boiling water to come halfway up sides of molds. Bake in 350°F oven about 30 minutes or until mixture feels firm. Stand 2 minutes before turning onto serving plates.

Combine water and juice in pan, bring to boil. Reduce heat, add oysters, simmer about 30 seconds or until oysters are opaque. Serve oysters with mousseline and saffron sauce.

Saffron Sauce: Melt butter in pan, add onion, cook, stirring, until soft. Add water, wine, crumbled bouillon cube and saffron, simmer, uncovered, 5 minutes. Stir in cream, simmer further 5 minutes. Strain sauce, return to pan. Stir in blended cornstarch and extra water, stir over high heat until sauce boils and thickens.

Serves 6.

■ Mousseline can be prepared 4 hours ahead. Sauce best made just before serving.
■ Storage: Covered, in refrigerator.
■ Freeze: Not suitable.
■ Microwave: Not suitable.

SMOKED TROUT SOUFFLE IN VOL AU VENT CASES

1 small smoked trout
3 tablespoons butter
2 tablespoons all-purpose flour
¼ teaspoon dry mustard
1 cup milk
3 eggs, separated
4 teaspoons grated Parmesan cheese
3 tablespoons chopped fresh dill
1 egg white, extra
4 x 4 inch packaged vol au vent cases

Remove flesh from trout, chop finely; you need 1 cup trout for this recipe. Melt butter in pan, add flour and mustard, cook, stirring, 1 minute.

Remove from heat, gradually stir in milk, stir over high heat until mixture boils and thickens. Transfer mixture to large bowl, stand 5 minutes. Stir in egg yolks, trout, cheese and dill. Beat all 4 egg whites in small bowl until soft peaks form, fold into warm trout mixture. Place vol au vent cases onto baking sheet, divide mixture between cases. Bake in 375°F oven about 20 minutes or until risen and lightly browned. Serve immediately.

Serves 4.

■ Make recipe just before serving.
■ Freeze: Not suitable.
■ Microwave: Souffle mixture suitable.

ABOVE: Scallop Mousseline with Saffron Sauce.
RIGHT: Smoked Trout Souffle in Vol au Vent Case.

SEAFOOD ANTIPASTI

2oz thinly sliced prosciutto
½ small cantaloupe, chopped
½lb mussels, cooked
10oz cooked jumbo shrimp, shelled
lettuce

PICKLED OCTOPUS
1lb baby octopus
⅔ cup white wine vinegar
2 cloves garlic, minced
4 teaspoons chopped fresh mint
1 teaspoon sugar

CAULIFLOWER SALAD
¼ medium cauliflower, chopped
4oz can diced red bell pepper, drained
1½oz can anchovy fillets, drained
2 teaspoons drained capers
3 tablespoons olive oil
4 teaspoons fresh lemon juice
4 teaspoons chopped fresh parsley

MARINATED OLIVES
¼lb black olives
¼lb green olives
⅓ cup olive oil
4 teaspoons salad oil
3 tablespoons fresh lemon juice
1 clove garlic, minced
3 tablespoons chopped fresh basil
½ teaspoon dried oregano leaves
1 small fresh red chili pepper,
**   finely chopped**

Cut prosciutto into strips large enough to wrap around the pieces of cantaloupe. Arrange mussels, shrimp, wrapped cantaloupe pieces, lettuce, octopus, cauliflower salad and olives on large serving plate.

Pickled Octopus: Remove and discard heads from octopus, place octopus in large pan, cover with water, simmer, covered, 1 hour; drain. Cut octopus into pieces, combine in bowl with vinegar, garlic, mint and sugar; cover, refrigerate.

Cauliflower Salad: Boil, steam or microwave cauliflower until just tender, drain, rinse under cold water; drain well. Combine cauliflower, pepper, anchovies and capers in bowl, add oil, juice and parsley; cover, refrigerate several hours.

Marinated Olives: Cut several small slits in each olive, combine in jar with oils, juice, garlic, herbs and chili pepper; cover, refrigerate several days before using.

Serves 8 to 10.

■ Octopus can be pickled 5 days ahead. Cauliflower salad can be made a day ahead. Olives can made 3 weeks ahead. Arrange antipasti on platter as close to serving time as possible.
■ Storage: Covered, in refrigerator.
■ Freeze: Not suitable.
■ Microwave: Not suitable.

LEFT: Seafood Antipasti.

SALMON RICE PUFF WITH MUSTARD BUTTER SAUCE

2 large spinach leaves
1 Atlantic salmon cutlet
1 tablespoon butter
1 small red bell pepper,
   finely chopped
¾ cup cooked rice
1 sheet (10in x 10in) ready rolled
   puff pastry
1 hard-boiled egg, chopped
1 egg, lightly beaten

MUSTARD BUTTER SAUCE
4 teaspoons fresh lemon juice
1 teaspoon seeded mustard
½ cup (1 stick) butter, chopped
4 teaspoons chopped fresh dill

Boil, steam or microwave spinach until just tender, drain. Press excess liquid from spinach; chop, cool.

Poach fish in shallow pan of water until just cooked; drain, cool. Chop fish finely.

Heat butter in skillet, add pepper, cook, stirring, until soft. Transfer to bowl, stir in spinach and rice. Cut pastry sheet in half, place half on lightly greased baking sheet, top with rice mixture, leaving ¼ inch border. Sprinkle fish and hard-boiled egg over rice mixture, brush edges with lightly beaten egg. Top with remaining pastry, press edges together with fork. Brush all over with lightly beaten egg, bake in 400°F oven about 25 minutes or until golden brown. Serve with hot sauce.

Mustard Butter Sauce: Combine juice and mustard in bowl over pan of simmering water. Gradually whisk in pieces of butter over heat, whisk until thick; stir in dill.

Serves 4.

- Rice filling can be made 2 days ahead. Assembled puff and sauce best cooked just before serving.
- Freeze: Not suitable.
- Microwave: Not suitable.

SEAFOOD AND CHICKEN RICE

14oz small mussels
4 teaspoons olive oil
1 large boneless, skinless chicken
   breast half, chopped
3 tablespoons olive oil, extra
1 onion, chopped
1 clove garlic, minced
1 small red bell pepper, chopped
1 small green bell pepper, chopped
2 slices bacon, chopped
½ cup frozen green peas
2½ cups water
½ small chicken bouillon cube
¾ cup rice
1lb cooked shrimp, shelled

Scrub mussels, remove beards, cook mussels in pan of boiling water about 4 minutes or until shells open. Remove and discard 1 shell from each mussel.

Heat oil in wok or skillet, add chicken, stir-fry until lightly browned and just cooked, remove from wok.

Heat extra oil in wok, add onion, garlic, peppers, bacon and peas, stir-fry until onion is soft. Add water and crumbled bouillon cube, bring to boil, gradually add rice, reduce heat, cover, cook over low heat about 20 minutes or until rice is tender and liquid absorbed. Add mussels, chicken and shrimp to pan, stir gently over medium heat until seafood and chicken are heated through.

Serves 8.

- Recipe best made just before serving.
- Freeze: Not suitable.
- Microwave: Not suitable.

RIGHT: Salmon Rice Puff with Mustard Butter Sauce.
LEFT: Seafood and Chicken Rice.

JELLIED WINE AND SEAFOOD RING

½lb fresh asparagus spears
1 cooked lobster
1 large Atlantic salmon cutlet
3 tablespoons unflavored gelatin
¼ cup water
2 cups apple juice
1¾ cups dry white wine
1lb cooked jumbo shrimp, shelled
fresh dill sprigs
2 teaspoons drained green
   peppercorns

Boil, steam or microwave asparagus until just tender; drain.

Remove lobster flesh from shell, cut flesh into slices. Cut fish into 1¼ inch pieces, poach in simmering water about 2 minutes or until just cooked, drain; cool. Cover, refrigerate 30 minutes.

Sprinkle gelatin over water in bowl, stand in pan of simmering water, stir until dissolved. Stir in warmed apple juice and wine, cool to room temperature, do not allow to set.

Pour 1 cup of the wine jelly mixture into 9 inch savarin ring pan, cover, refrigerate until set. Place asparagus in pan, gently pour in enough wine jelly mixture to just cover asparagus, refrigerate until set. Repeat layering and refrigerating with wine mixture, shrimp, lobster, fish, dill and peppercorns.

Serves 4 to 6.

- Recipe can be made a day ahead.
- Storage: Covered, in refrigerator.
- Freeze: Not suitable.
- Microwave: Gelatin suitable.

BELOW: Jellied Wine and Seafood Ring.
RIGHT: Fish Puffs With Lemon Hollandaise.

FISH PUFFS WITH LEMON HOLLANDAISE

¼ cup packaged unseasoned
    bread crumbs
½lb white fish fillets, chopped
½ cup fresh white bread crumbs
⅓ cup sour cream
2 teaspoons anchovy sauce
½ teaspoon tabasco sauce
1 teaspoon grated lemon zest
3 tablespoons chopped fresh chives
2 eggs, separated
2 egg whites, extra
3 tablespoons grated Parmesan
    cheese

LEMON HOLLANDAISE
2 egg yolks
½ teaspoon grated lemon zest
2 tablespoons fresh lemon juice
3oz (¾ stick) butter, melted

Grease 4 souffle dishes (½ cup capacity), sprinkle inside with packaged bread crumbs; shake away excess crumbs.

Process fish until smooth, add fresh bread crumbs, sour cream, sauces, zest, chives and egg yolks, process until combined. Transfer mixture to bowl.

Beat egg whites and extra egg whites until firm peaks form. Fold into fish mixture. Spoon mixture evenly into prepared dishes, sprinkle with cheese. Bake in 375°F oven about 20 minutes. Serve with lemon hollandaise.

Lemon Hollandaise: Blend or process egg yolks, zest and juice until combined. While motor is operating, gradually add hot, bubbling butter in thin stream, blend until thick.

Serves 4.

■ Puffs and hollandaise best made
    just before serving.
■ Freeze: Not suitable.
■ Microwave: Not suitable.

DEEP-FRIED OYSTERS WITH AVOCADO SAUCE

18 oysters
all-purpose flour
1 egg, lightly beaten
3 tablespoons milk
1½ cups packaged unseasoned
**   bread crumbs**
oil for deep-frying
3 tablespoons sour cream
1oz black lumpfish caviar

AVOCADO SAUCE
1 small avocado
1 green onion, chopped
4 teaspoons fresh lemon juice
4 teaspoons water
1 clove garlic, minced

Remove and discard top shell from each oyster, remove oysters from shells. Toss oysters in flour, dip in combined egg and milk, then bread crumbs. Deep-fry in hot oil until lightly browned; drain on absorbent paper. Serve oysters in half shells with avocado sauce, sour cream and caviar.

Avocado Sauce: Blend or process all ingredients until smooth.

Serves 6.

■ Recipe best made just before serving.
■ Freeze: Not suitable.
■ Microwave: Not suitable.

SEAFOOD WITH GINGERROOT WINE BUTTER

18 uncooked jumbo shrimp, shelled
18 sea scallops

GINGERROOT WINE BUTTER
3oz (¾ stick) butter
2 teaspoons grated fresh gingerroot
1 clove garlic, minced
¼ cup dry white wine
4 teaspoons chopped fresh parsley
4 teaspoons chopped fresh chives

Cut almost through backs of shrimp, remove dark vein. Press shrimp open gently along cut side with knife. Wrap a shrimp around each scallop. Secure with toothpicks, brush with gingerroot wine butter, broil until just cooked, brush with the butter during cooking. Remove toothpicks before serving.

Gingerroot Wine Butter: Melt butter, add juice from gingerroot (do this by pressing gingerroot between two spoons or in garlic press). Add garlic, wine and herbs. Bring to boil before using.

Serves 6.

- Shrimp and butter can be prepared 3 hours ahead; broil just before serving.
- Storage: Shrimp, covered, in refrigerator.
- Freeze: Not suitable.
- Microwave: Not suitable.

ABOVE: Deep-Fried Oysters with Avocado Sauce.
RIGHT: Seafood with Gingerroot Wine Butter.

LOBSTER AND FISH TIMBALES WITH LIME SAUCE

1 large uncooked lobster tail
2 tablespoons (¼ stick) butter
2 green onions, chopped
⅓ cup dry white wine
5oz white fish fillets, chopped
½ cup fresh white bread crumbs
1 cup heavy cream
1 teaspoon grated lime zest
3 eggs, separated

LIME SAUCE
1 lime
¾ cup water
¼ cup dry white wine
¼ cup heavy cream
1 small chicken bouillon cube
½ cup (1 stick) butter, chopped

Remove lobster flesh from shell; chop roughly. Heat butter in skillet, add onions, cook, stirring, until just soft. Add wine, simmer, uncovered, 1 minute.

Process lobster, fish, onion mixture, bread crumbs, cream, zest and egg yolks until well combined. Transfer mixture to bowl. Beat egg whites in bowl until soft peaks form, gently fold into seafood mixture. Spoon mixture into 8 greased timbale molds (½ cup capacity), cover with foil, place in roasting pan, pour in enough boiling water to come halfway up sides of molds. Bake in 350°F oven about 30 minutes or until just set. Stand 3 minutes, turn onto plates. Serve with sauce.

Lime Sauce: Cut peel thinly from lime using a vegetable peeler, cut into thin strips. Squeeze lime to make 3 tablespoons of juice for sauce. Combine water, wine, cream and crumbled bouillon cube in pan, bring to boil. Boil, uncovered, until liquid is reduced by half. Stir in juice and peel, remove from heat, gradually whisk in butter.

Serves 8.

■ Timbale mixture can be prepared several hours ahead. Lime sauce must be made just before serving.
■ Storage: Covered, in refrigerator.
■ Freeze: Not suitable.
■ Microwave: Not suitable.

BELOW: From left: Fish and Shrimp Quenelles with Orange Sauce; Lobster and Fish Timbales with Lime Sauce.
RIGHT: Seafood Banana Cocktail.

FISH AND SHRIMP QUENELLES WITH ORANGE SAUCE

½lb white fish fillets, chopped
½lb uncooked shrimp, shelled
2 egg whites
1 cup heavy cream
¼ teaspoon ground nutmeg

ORANGE SAUCE
4 teaspoons sugar
1 onion, chopped
1 cup fresh orange juice
1 small chicken bouillon cube
1 cup water
2 teaspoons cornstarch
4 teaspoons water, extra

Process all ingredients until smooth. Spread mixture evenly onto a flat tray, cover, refrigerate several hours or overnight until firm. Mold mixture into oval shapes using 2 small wet tablespoons. Spoon mixture into a pan of gently simmering water. Poach about 5 minutes on each side, it is important not to allow water

to come to the boil or quenelles will fall apart. Drain quenelles on absorbent paper. Serve with sauce.

Orange Sauce: Place sugar in pan over medium heat, cook, without stirring, until sugar is melted. Remove from heat, add onion, juice, crumbled bouillon cube and water, stir until pieces of toffee are dissolved. Simmer about 5 minutes or until reduced by one-third, strain, return to pan. Add blended cornstarch and extra water; stir over high heat until sauce boils and thickens slightly.

Serves 4.

■ Quenelle mixture can be made a day ahead. Sauce can be made 3 hours ahead.
■ Storage: Covered, in refrigerator.
■ Freeze: Not suitable.
■ Microwave: Not suitable.

SEAFOOD BANANA COCKTAIL

4 bananas, sliced
4 teaspoons fresh lemon juice
½ cup mayonnaise
6oz can crabmeat, drained
3½oz cooked shelled shrimp, chopped
4 teaspoons pine nuts
4 teaspoons chopped fresh dill

Combine bananas and juice in bowl, gently stir in mayonnaise, seafood, nuts and dill.

Serves 4.

■ Recipe best made just before serving.
■ Freeze: Not suitable.
■ Microwave: Not suitable.

SALMON FLOWERS WITH HERBED CREAM CHEESE

1 sheet (10in x 10in) ready rolled puff pastry
18 slices smoked salmon
18 drained capers

HERBED CREAM CHEESE
2oz cream cheese, softened
8oz container sour cream
4 teaspoons fresh lemon juice
4 teaspoons chopped fresh dill

Cut pastry into six 2½ inch x 4½ inch pieces. Place on baking sheet, bake in 400˚F oven about 8 minutes or until puffed and lightly browned; cool. Make flowers by gathering edges of slices of smoked salmon together, place on serving plates. Garnish with capers, serve with pastry rectangles and herbed cream cheese.
Herbed Cream Cheese: Beat cheese in bowl with electric mixer until soft; gradually beat in sour cream, beat until slightly thickened; stir in juice and dill.

Serves 6.

■ Recipe can be prepared a day ahead. Assemble just before serving.
■ Storage: Cheese, covered, in refrigerator. Puffs, in airtight container.
■ Freeze: Not suitable.
■ Microwave: Not suitable.

SHRIMP, MANGO AND AVOCADO SALAD

3 avocados
3 mangoes, peeled
1½lb cooked shrimp, shelled
5oz button mushrooms, sliced

DRESSING
1 teaspoon grated fresh gingerroot
½ cup light olive oil
3 tablespoons white wine vinegar
1½ teaspoons honey
1 teaspoon seeded mustard
1 tablespoon fresh lemon juice
4 teaspoons chopped fresh chives
1 teaspoon chopped fresh dill

Cut avocados in half lengthways. Remove flesh, reserve shells. Chop avocado into chunks. Chop mangoes and shrimp into pieces same size as the avocado. Combine avocado, mango, shrimp and mushrooms in bowl, add dressing, toss, serve in avocado shells.
Dressing: Squeeze gingerroot between 2 teaspoons or in garlic press to extract juice. Combine juice with remaining ingredients in jar; shake well.

Serves 6.

■ Salad best made close to serving.
■ Freeze: Not suitable.

RIGHT: Shrimp, Mango and Avocado Salad.
ABOVE: Salmon Flowers with Herbed Cream Cheese.
FAR RIGHT: From left: Shrimp Pie Puffs; Crab Waffles with Mild Curry Sauce.

SHRIMP PIE PUFFS

PASTRY
1 cup all-purpose flour
¼ cup (½ stick) butter, chopped
1 egg, lightly beaten
4 teaspoons water, approximately
**1 sheet (10in x 10in) ready rolled
    puff pastry**
1 egg yolk, extra

FILLING
2 tablespoons (¼ stick) butter
3½oz button mushrooms, sliced
3 green onions, chopped
**7oz uncooked shelled
    shrimp, chopped**
3 tablespoons all-purpose flour
¼ cup milk
3 tablespoons heavy cream
4 teaspoons chopped fresh parsley

Pastry: Sift flour into large bowl, rub in butter. Add egg and enough water to make ingredients cling together. Knead dough on lightly floured surface until smooth, cover, refrigerate 30 minutes. Roll pastry out thinly between baking paper into 9½ inch x 18 inch rectangle. Cut into 4½ inch rounds to line 8 x ⅓ cup muffin tins; lift into tins. Prick pastry bases with fork, refrigerate 20 minutes. Bake in 375°F oven about 15 minutes or until lightly browned; cool. Spoon filling into cases.

Cut 8 x 2½ inch rounds from puff pastry. Brush edges of pastry bases with a little water. Gently press pastry rounds on top; trim edges. Cut 2 small slits in top of each pie to allow steam to escape during cooking. Brush pies with extra egg

yolk. Bake in 375°F oven about 15 minutes or until golden brown.

Filling: Melt butter in pan, add mushrooms and onions, cook, stirring, 1 minute. Add shrimp, cook, stirring, about 2 minutes or until shrimp are just cooked. Add flour, cook, stirring, 1 minute. Remove from heat, gradually stir in milk and cream. Stir over high heat until mixture boils and thickens, add parsley; cool.

Makes 8.

■ Pies can be made a day ahead.
■ Storage: Covered, in refrigerator.
■ Freeze: Suitable.
■ Microwave: Not suitable.

CRAB WAFFLES WITH MILD CURRY SAUCE

¾ cup all-purpose flour
¼ cup self-rising flour
**3 tablespoons grated Parmesan
    cheese**
1 egg, separated
¾ cup milk
7oz canned crabmeat, drained, flaked
¼ cup (½ stick) butter, melted
¼ cup water

MILD CURRY SAUCE
2 teaspoons butter
2 green onions, chopped
2 teaspoons all-purpose flour
4 teaspoons curry powder
¼ teaspoon ground cumin
¾ cup milk
¼ cup pineapple juice
4 teaspoons sour cream
2 teaspoons chopped fresh cilantro

Sift flours into bowl, stir in cheese, gradually stir in combined egg yolk, milk and crabmeat. Add butter and water, stir until smooth. Beat egg whites until soft peaks form, fold into crab mixture. Drop about 3 heaped tablespoons of mixture onto heated greased waffle iron. Close iron, cook about 2 minutes or until golden brown. Serve with sauce.

Mild Curry Sauce: Melt butter in pan, add onions, cook, stirring, until soft. Stir in flour, curry powder and cumin, cook, stirring, 1 minute. Remove from heat, gradually stir in milk and juice, stir over high heat until mixture boils and thickens. Strain; stir in sour cream and cilantro.

Serves 6.

■ Waffles best made close to serving. Sauce can be made 3 days ahead.
■ Storage: Covered, in refrigerator.
■ Freeze: Cooked waffles suitable; reheat in 350°F oven.
■ Microwave: Sauce suitable.

CHILI PASTA WITH CREAMY SHRIMP SAUCE

We made our own pasta for this recipe, but any fresh or dried pasta of your choice will suit this sauce. You will need to buy ½lb fresh pasta to serve 4.

CHILI PASTA
1 cup all-purpose flour
1 egg, lightly beaten
4 teaspoons olive oil
2 tablespoons chili powder
3 tablespoons water

CREAMY SHRIMP SAUCE
1lb uncooked shrimp
2 cups heavy cream
1 clove garlic, minced
¼ cup fresh lemon juice
4 teaspoons cornstarch
3 tablespoons water

Chili Pasta: Process all ingredients until combined. Turn dough onto lightly floured surface, knead about 5 minutes or until smooth. Make pasta following your pasta machine's directions. Add pasta gradually to large pan of boiling water, boil, un-covered, until just tender, drain. Serve pasta with creamy shrimp sauce.

Creamy Shrimp Sauce: Shell and devein shrimp; wash and reserve shells. Combine shrimp shells, cream, garlic and juice in pan. Simmer, uncovered, about 5 minutes or until reduced by about one-third. Strain sauce, return to pan, stir in blended cornstarch and water, stir over high heat until sauce boils and thickens. Add shrimp, heat without boiling, about 3 minutes or until shrimp change color.

Serves 4.

- ■ Sauce is best made just before serving.
- ■ Freeze: Not suitable.
- ■ Microwave: Pasta suitable.

RIGHT: Chili Pasta with Creamy Shrimp Sauce.

58

Appetizers
Poultry

With chicken, turkey, duck and quail, you can enjoy tempting and different appetizers. As well as fresh and frozen poultry, we used some smoked poultry for a tasty change. These appetizers are ideal to serve with seafood as a main course and some would also make ideal light meals or ritzy snacks.

CHICKEN MANGO SALAD WITH ORANGE MINT DRESSING

1 small chicken bouillon cube
2 cups water
2 boneless, skinless chicken
    breast halves
2 mangoes, sliced
1 lettuce

ORANGE MINT DRESSING
½ cup chopped fresh mint
½ cup olive oil
½ cup fresh orange juice
½ teaspoon superfine sugar

Combine crumbled bouillon cube and water in pan, bring to boil, add chicken. reduce heat, poach chicken about 3 minutes on each side or until just cooked. Drain chicken, cool; cut into slices.

Serve chicken with mangoes and lettuce; pour orange mint dressing over salad just before serving.
Orange Mint Dressing: Combine all ingredients in jar; shake well.

Serves 4.

■ Salad is best made just before serving.
■ Freeze: Not suitable.
■ Microwave: Suitable.

SPICY CHICKEN SAUSAGE WITH SAFFRON CREAM

4 teaspoons olive oil
1 onion, chopped
1 clove garlic, minced
14oz ground chicken
1 egg white
1 teaspoon sambal oelek
¼ teaspoon chili powder
¼ teaspoon ground cumin
¾ cup fresh white bread crumbs

SAFFRON CREAM
1 teaspoon butter
1 teaspoon all-purpose flour
2 green onions, chopped
3 tablespoons dry white wine
½ cup heavy cream
½ small chicken bouillon cube
tiny pinch saffron powder
1 teaspoon chopped fresh parsley

Heat oil in pan, add onion and garlic, cook, stirring, until onion is soft. Process onion mixture, chicken, egg white, sambal oelek, chili powder and cumin until smooth. Transfer to bowl, stir in bread crumbs. Divide mixture in half. Spread half the mixture onto a piece of plastic wrap, roll into sausage shape about 1½ inches in diameter.

Repeat with remaining mixture. Wrap each roll in foil, poach in shallow pan of simmering water 15 minutes. Remove from water; cool, refrigerate several hours or overnight. Serve sliced sausages with saffron cream.
Saffron Cream: Blend butter with flour in cup using teaspoon. Combine green onions and wine in pan, simmer until almost all liquid has evaporated. Stir in cream, crumbled bouillon cube and saffron. Stir in blended butter and flour, stir over high heat until mixture boils and thickens, strain; stir in parsley.

Serves 6 to 8.

■ Sausages can be made 3 days
   ahead. Saffron cream best made
   just before serving.
■ Storage: Covered, in refrigerator.
■ Freeze: Sausages suitable.
■ Microwave: Not suitable.

RIGHT: From top: Spicy Chicken Sausage with Saffron Cream; Chicken Mango Salad with Orange Mint Dressing.

BROILED QUAIL WITH BRAISED LEEK RIBBONS

3 quail
4 teaspoons light soy sauce
4 teaspoons honey
4 teaspoons light olive oil
1 clove garlic, minced
ground rock salt
ground black pepper

BRAISED LEEK RIBBONS
2 small leeks
3oz (¾ stick) butter

Remove necks from quail. Using knife or sharp pair of scissors, cut along backbone round to breast bone. Combine sauce, honey, oil and garlic in bowl. Brush mixture over quail, stand 2 hours or refrigerate, covered, overnight. Sprinkle skin of quail with salt and pepper. Broil quail on both sides until cooked. Serve quail with leek ribbons.

Braised Leek Ribbons: Cut leeks into quarters lengthways. Heat butter in skillet, add leeks, cover, cook over very low heat about 15 minutes or until tender, stirring mixture occasionally.

Serves 6.

- ▣ Quail can be prepared a day ahead. Cook quail and leeks just before serving.
- ▣ Storage: Covered, in refrigerator.
- ▣ Freeze: Not suitable.
- ▣ Microwave: Not suitable.

CHICKEN SALAD WITH CUCUMBER DRESSING

1 small chicken bouillon cube
2 cups water
2 boneless, skinless chicken
    breast halves
lettuce

CUCUMBER DRESSING
½ cup fresh lemon juice
3 tablespoons salad oil
4 teaspoons walnut oil
4 teaspoons chopped fresh tarragon
1 clove garlic, minced
1 teaspoon grated fresh gingerroot
¼ small green cucumber,
    seeded, chopped
½ small red bell pepper, chopped
2 green onions, chopped

Combine crumbled bouillon cube and water in pan, bring to boil, reduce heat, add chicken. Simmer about 10 minutes or until chicken is cooked through; drain, cool. Serve sliced chicken on lettuce; spoon over dressing.

Cucumber Dressing: Blend juice, oils, tarragon, garlic and gingerroot until smooth. Combine remaining ingredients in bowl, stir in juice mixture. Cover, refrigerate until cold.

Serves 4.

- ▣ Recipe can be prepared several hours before serving.
- ▣ Storage: Covered, in refrigerator.
- ▣ Freeze: Not suitable.
- ▣ Microwave: Suitable.

QUAIL BREASTS WITH PORT WINE SAUCE

6 quail
all-purpose flour
3 tablespoons light olive oil
¼ cup sour cream, approximately

PORT WINE SAUCE
3 tablespoons light olive oil
1 onion, chopped
1 small stalk celery, chopped
3 tablespoons all-purpose flour
½ cup port wine
3 cups water
⅛ teaspoon dried thyme leaves
6 fresh parsley stems
4 teaspoons Worcestershire sauce

PARSNIP CHIPS
2 parsnips
oil for deep-frying

Use small sharp knife to remove breast and wing from quail in 1 piece. Cut carefully around rib cage on 1 side, repeat with other side. Remove wing tips. Reserve bodies for sauce.

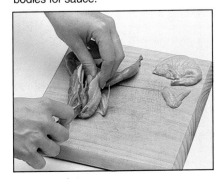

Dust quail breasts lightly with flour, shake away excess flour. Heat oil in skillet, add breasts skin-side-down, cook until browned and cooked through. Pour sauce onto serving plate, add sour cream, top with quail; serve with parsnip chips.

Port Wine Sauce: Heat oil in pan, add onion, celery and reserved quail bodies, cook, stirring, until ingredients are well browned. Stir in flour, cook, stirring, until flour mixture is lightly browned. Remove from heat, gradually stir in wine, water, thyme, parsley and sauce. Stir over high heat until mixture boils and thickens, simmer, uncovered, 1 hour. Strain sauce. Reheat, if necessary, before serving.

Parsnip Chips: Use a vegetable peeler to peel thin strips from parsnips. Deep-fry strips in hot oil until lightly browned; drain on absorbent paper.

Serves 4.

- ▣ Sauce can be made a day ahead. Quail breasts and parsnip chips best cooked just before serving.
- ▣ Storage: Covered, in refrigerator.
- ▣ Freeze: Not suitable.
- ▣ Microwave: Not suitable.

ABOVE: Quail Breasts with Port Wine Sauce.
LEFT: From top: Chicken Salad with Cucumber Dressing; Broiled Quail with Braised Leek Ribbons.

Sesame Marinade: Combine all ingredients in bowl.

Serves 6.

- Salad can be prepared several hours ahead.
- Storage: Covered, in refrigerator.
- Freeze: Not suitable.
- Microwave: Not suitable.

SQUAB WITH SWEET ONION RELISH

2 x 7oz squab
¼lb slices bacon
1 tablespoon butter

SWEET ONION RELISH
1 tablespoon butter
1 large red onion, thinly sliced
1 large white onion, thinly sliced
¼ cup red wine vinegar
¼ cup water
3 tablespoons honey
4 teaspoons chopped fresh chives

Cut squab in half lengthways, flatten slightly. Cut bacon in half lengthways. Place squab breast-side-down on broiler tray, brush with butter, broil until almost cooked. Turn, wrap with bacon, broil until lightly browned and cooked through. Serve with warm or cold onion relish.

Sweet Onion Relish: Melt butter in skillet, add onions, cook, stirring, until onions are soft. Stir in vinegar, water and honey, simmer, uncovered, about 10 minutes or until liquid is reduced to about half; stir occasionally. Add chives to relish mixture.

Serves 4.

- Squab are best cooked just before serving. Relish can be made several days ahead.
- Storage: Covered, in refrigerator.
- Freeze: Not suitable.
- Microwave: Not suitable.

DUCK BREASTS WITH RED CURRANT SAUCE

4 duck breasts
all-purpose flour
1 tablespoon butter

RED CURRANT SAUCE
⅓ cup red currant jelly
⅓ cup water
4 teaspoons grated orange zest
1 teaspoon French mustard
2 teaspoons cornstarch
2 teaspoons water, extra
2 green onions, finely chopped
3 tablespoons port wine

Remove skin from duck. Place skin on wire rack in roasting pan, bake in 375°F oven 10 minutes or until crisp; cool. Toss duck in flour, shake away excess. Heat butter in skillet, add duck, cook about 1½ minutes on each side or until cooked through; drain on absorbent paper. Slice duck and skin, serve with sauce.

Red Currant Sauce: Combine jelly, water, zest and mustard in pan, bring to boil, boil, uncovered, 2 minutes. Stir in blended cornstarch and extra water, stir over high heat until sauce boils and thickens. Stir in green onions and wine.

Serves 4.

- Sauce can be made a day ahead.
- Storage: Covered, in refrigerator.
- Freeze: Not suitable.
- Microwave: Not suitable.

ROAST DUCK SALAD WITH WILD RICE

¼ cup wild rice
1 Chinese roasted duck
3 tablespoons watercress sprigs

SESAME MARINADE
4 teaspoons fresh lemon juice
2 teaspoons Oriental sesame oil
2 teaspoons dark soy sauce
½ teaspoon sugar

Add rice to pan of boiling water, boil, uncovered, about 25 minutes or until rice is tender; drain. Remove skin from duck, place skin on wire rack in roasting pan, bake in 375°F oven 10 minutes or until crisp. Cool, cut into thin strips. Remove meat from duck, cut into thin strips. Place meat in bowl with marinade, cover, refrigerate 2 hours or overnight. Remove from marinade, add rice and watercress to marinade. Serve duck with skin strips, rice mixture and salad vegetables.

RIGHT: Squab with Sweet Onion Relish.
ABOVE: From top: Duck Breasts with Red Currant Sauce; Roast Duck Salad with Wild Rice.

MARINATED QUAIL WITH BASIL MUSTARD SAUCE

4 quail
½ cup white wine Worcestershire sauce
3 tablespoons walnut oil
3 tablespoons fresh lemon juice
12 spears fresh asparagus
12 snow peas

BASIL MUSTARD SAUCE
3 tablespoons sour cream
3 tablespoons chopped fresh basil
1 teaspoon French mustard

Using scissors, cut down both sides of backbone of all quail. Remove and discard backbones.

Use heel of hand to press quail flat.

Tuck wings under bodies. Place quail in large bowl with sauce, oil and juice, mix well. Cover, refrigerate mixture several hours or overnight.

Remove quail from marinade, reserve marinade. Broil quail about 5 minutes on each side or until cooked as desired, basting frequently with marinade.

Boil, steam or microwave asparagus and snow peas until just tender, serve with warm quail; top quail with sauce.

Basil Mustard Sauce: Place remaining reserved marinade in pan, bring to boil; cool 5 minutes. Stir in sour cream, basil and mustard; mix well.

Serves 4.

- ■ Recipe can be prepared a day ahead; cook just before serving.
- ■ Storage: Covered, in refrigerator.
- ■ Freeze: Marinated quail suitable.
- ■ Microwave: Vegetables suitable.

RIGHT: Marinated Quail with Basil Mustard Sauce.

SMOKED TURKEY AND BERRY SALAD

½ small bunch chicory
¼lb sliced smoked turkey
2 small green cucumbers
1 onion, thinly sliced
½ cup blueberries
½ cup red currants
½ cup walnut pieces

DRESSING
¼ cup walnut oil
2 tablespoons raspberry vinegar
½ teaspoon sugar
1 clove garlic, minced

Chop chicory roughly, cut turkey and cucumbers into thin strips. Combine chicory, turkey, cucumbers, onion, berries, currants and walnuts in bowl, toss gently. Top with dressing just before serving.
Dressing: Combine all ingredients in jar; shake well.

Serves 4.

■ Salad best made close to serving.
■ Freeze: Not suitable.

CRAB SEASONED CHICKEN WINGS

4 large chicken wings
4 teaspoons hoisin sauce
4 teaspoons honey
4 teaspoons dry sherry
½ teaspoon Oriental sesame oil
4 teaspoons sesame seeds

CRAB SEASONING
4 teaspoons light olive oil
¼ teaspoon Oriental sesame oil
1 onion, finely chopped
1 clove garlic, minced
¼ cup grated carrot
1 small red bell pepper, finely chopped
½ teaspoon grated fresh gingerroot
6oz can crabmeat, drained
1 tablespoon light soy sauce

Without cutting through skin, cut chicken flesh away from bones down to the first joint. Pull flesh back over joint, remove bone at joint. Cut flesh away from joint to expose smaller bones.

Pull flesh back over the two smaller bones and remove bones at next joint with knife, return chicken wing to normal shape ready for filling.
Fill boned wings with crab seasoning; secure openings with toothpicks.

Place seasoned wings into roasting pan, top with combined sauce, honey, sherry and sesame oil. Sprinkle wings with sesame seeds, bake in 375°F oven about 25 minutes or until chicken is cooked through. Brush wings with pan juices during cooking.
Crab Seasoning: Heat oils in skillet, add onion and garlic, cook, stirring, until onion is soft. Add carrot, pepper and gingerroot to pan, cook, stirring, further minute. Stir in crabmeat and sauce; cool mixure slightly before using.

Serves 4.

■ Wings can be boned and filled a day ahead.
■ Storage: Covered, in refrigerator.
■ Freeze: Not suitable.
■ Microwave: Not suitable.

HERBED SMOKED CHICKEN ON POTATO CAKES

1 cup water
1 small chicken bouillon cube
¼ cup fresh orange juice
4 teaspoons cornstarch
4 teaspoons water, extra
3 tablespoons chopped fresh parsley
4 teaspoons chopped fresh chives
2 teaspoons chopped fresh cilantro
2lb smoked chicken

POTATO CAKES
2 medium potatoes
3 tablespoons olive oil
2 tablespoons (¼ stick) butter

Combine water, crumbled bouillon cube and juice in pan, simmer 2 minutes. Stir in blended cornstarch and extra water, stir over heat until mixture boils and thickens; add herbs. Remove chicken meat from bones, slice meat thinly. Add chicken to pan, stir until heated through, serve chicken over warm potato cakes.
Potato Cakes: Boil, steam or microwave unpeeled potatoes until just cooked; drain. Peel potatoes, cover, refrigerate 1 hour. Coarsely grate potatoes, divide into 6 portions, shape into flat cakes. Heat oil and butter in skillet, add cakes, cook until lightly browned underneath. Turn, brown other side; drain on absorbent paper.

Serves 6.

■ Recipe best made just before serving.
■ Freeze: Not suitable.
■ Microwave: Chicken mixture suitable.

BACON AND FRESH HERB SEASONED DRUMSTICKS

6 chicken drumsticks
oil for deep-frying

SEASONING
6 thin slices bacon
1 boneless, skinless chicken breast half, chopped
1 clove garlic, minced
3 tablespoons chopped fresh parsley
4 teaspoons chopped fresh chives
2 teaspoons chopped fresh cilantro

Using sharp knife, scrape flesh down bone of drumstick, working towards narrow end. As you do this, the meat will turn inside out.

Cut across bone, leaving flesh attached to knuckle at narrow end. Turn meat again so that skin is on the outside.

Spoon bacon and herb seasoning firmly into cavities of drumsticks.

Secure filled end with toothpicks. Tie bacon rinds, reserved from seasoning, around narrow end of drumsticks, forming a bow. Repeat with remaining drumsticks and seasoning.

Refrigerate 1 hour; deep-fry in hot oil about 6 minutes or until golden brown and cooked through.

Seasoning: Remove rind from bacon, reserve rind; chop bacon roughly. Blend or process all ingredients together until finely minced.

Makes 6.

- Seasoned drumsticks can be prepared a day ahead; deep-fry just before serving.
- Storage: Covered, in refrigerator.
- Freeze: Uncooked seasoned drumsticks suitable.
- Microwave: Not suitable.

BELOW: Clockwise from left: Herbed Smoked Chicken on Potato Cakes; Bacon and Fresh Herb Seasoned Drumsticks; Crab Seasoned Chicken Wings.
FAR RIGHT: Smoked Turkey and Berry Salad.

CHICKEN ROLLS WITH ORANGE GINGERROOT GLAZE

2 boneless, skinless chicken breast halves
2 tablespoons (¼ stick) butter
1 clove garlic, minced
1 teaspoon grated fresh gingerroot
1 teaspoon grated orange zest
3 tablespoons dried currants
7oz ground pork and veal
1 cup fresh white bread crumbs

ORANGE GINGERROOT GLAZE
2 teaspoons cornstarch
½ cup water
½ cup fresh orange juice
4 teaspoons chopped glace gingerroot
4 teaspoons sugar

Place chicken between pieces of plastic wrap; pound until thin. Melt butter in skillet, add garlic, gingerroot, zest and currants, cook, stirring, 1 minute. Add pork and veal, cook, stirring, until well browned. Remove from heat, stir in bread crumbs. Spread meat mixture evenly over each chicken breast, roll breasts up from a long side. Wrap each roll tightly in greased foil. Place rolls onto baking sheet, bake in 350°F oven about 40 minutes or until cooked through.

Stand rolls in foil 5 minutes before unwrapping. Serve sliced rolls with glaze.
Orange Gingerroot Glaze: Blend cornstarch with water in pan, stir in remaining ingredients, stir over high heat until mixture boils and thickens.

Serves 4.

- Chicken can be rolled several hours ahead. Sauce can be made a day ahead.
- Storage: Covered, in refrigerator.
- Freeze: Not suitable.
- Microwave: Glaze suitable.

ALMOND CHICKEN WITH CRANBERRY ORANGE SAUCE

½lb chicken tenderloins
all-purpose flour
1 egg, lightly beaten
4 teaspoons milk
½ cup packaged ground almonds
⅔ cup fresh white bread crumbs
2 teaspoons grated orange zest
oil for deep-frying

CRANBERRY ORANGE SAUCE
⅔ cup cranberry sauce
3 tablespoons fresh orange juice
1 teaspoon cornstarch
4 teaspoons water

Cut chicken into thin strips, toss in flour, shake away excess flour. Dip into combined egg and milk, then in combined almonds, bread crumbs and zest. Refrigerate 1 hour. Deep-fry chicken in hot oil until lightly browned, drain on absorbent paper. Serve with hot sauce.
Cranberry Orange Sauce: Combine all ingredients in pan, stir over heat until sauce boils and thickens.

Serves 4.

- Chicken can be crumbed several hours ahead. Cook chicken and sauce just before serving.
- Storage: Covered, in refrigerator.
- Freeze: Not suitable.
- Microwave: Not suitable.

SMOKED CHICKEN WITH MIXED PICKLE RELISH

½lb package fine egg noodles
2lb smoked chicken
4 Chinese dried mushrooms

MIXED PICKLE RELISH
⅓ cup drained Chinese mixed pickles, finely chopped
4 teaspoons oyster-flavored sauce
3 tablespoons sake

Add noodles to large pan of boiling water, boil, uncovered, until just tender. Drain, rinse under cold water, drain well; cool. Remove and discard skin and bones from chicken; thinly slice meat. Place mushrooms in small bowl, cover with hot water, stand 20 minutes; drain. Remove and discard stems from mushrooms; finely slice caps. Serve chicken and noodles with mushrooms and relish.
Mixed Pickle Relish: Combine all ingredients in small bowl.

Serves 4.

- Recipe can be prepared several hours ahead; cook noodles just before serving.
- Storage: Covered, in refrigerator.
- Freeze: Not suitable.
- Microwave: Noodles suitable.

RIGHT: Smoked Chicken with Mixed Pickle Relish.
ABOVE: From Left: Chicken Rolls with Orange Gingerroot Glaze; Almond Chicken with Cranberry Orange Sauce.

CHICKEN AND FRESH THYME ROULADE

¼ cup (½ stick) butter
⅓ cup all-purpose flour
1 cup milk
4 eggs, separated
½ cup chopped fresh parsley
4 teaspoons chopped fresh thyme

CHICKEN FILLING
1lb boneless, skinless chicken
   breasts
1½ cups water
¼ cup dry white wine
1 bay leaf
sprigs fresh thyme
1 small chicken bouillon cube
2 tablespoons (¼ stick) butter
3 tablespoons all-purpose flour
¼ cup heavy cream
½ cup fresh white bread crumbs

Grease 10 inch x 12 inch jelly-roll pan, line base with baking paper, grease paper.

Melt butter in pan, add flour, cook, stirring, 1 minute. Remove from heat, gradually stir in milk, stir over heat until mixture boils and thickens. Transfer to bowl. Stir in egg yolks and herbs. Beat egg whites in bowl until soft peaks form, fold into herb mixture in 2 batches.

Spread mixture into prepared pan; bake in 375°F oven about 15 minutes or until puffed and lightly browned. Turn onto wire rack covered with kitchen towel. Carefully remove lining paper; cool to room temperature, spread with filling, roll up like a jelly-roll, from long side, using towel to guide the roll. Cut into slices.

Chicken Filling: Combine chicken, water, wine, bay leaf, thyme and crumbled bouillon cube in pan, simmer, covered, until chicken is just cooked. Remove chicken from pan, chop finely. Bring liquid to boil, boil rapidly, uncovered, 5 minutes; strain, reserve ½ cup of the liquid; discard remaining liquid.

Melt butter in pan, add flour, cook, stirring, 1 minute. Remove from heat, stir in the ½ cup of reserved liquid and cream. Stir over high heat until mixture boils and thickens. Stir in chopped chicken and bread crumbs.

Serves 6 to 8.

- Roulade can be made several hours ahead; reheat, covered with foil, in 350°F oven about 15 minutes.
- Storage: Covered, in refrigerator.
- Freeze: Not suitable.
- Microwave: Roulade mixture and filling suitable.

CHICKEN CROQUETTES WITH PIQUANT SAUCE

2oz fine egg noodles
¼ cup dry instant mashed potato
¼ cup boiling water
1 onion, grated
1 clove garlic, minced
1 cup (7oz) finely chopped
   cooked chicken
1 cup (5oz) finely chopped
   mozzarella cheese
3 tablespoons grated Parmesan
   cheese
1 egg, lightly beaten
3 tablespoons chopped fresh chives
all-purpose flour
2 eggs, lightly beaten, extra
⅓ cup milk
packaged unseasoned bread crumbs
oil for deep-frying

PIQUANT SAUCE
1 tablespoon butter
6 green onions, chopped
1½ cups dry white wine
½ cup white vinegar
2 dill pickles, finely chopped
2 teaspoons chopped fresh parsley
2 teaspoons chopped fresh tarragon
1 small chicken bouillon cube
4 teaspoons all-purpose flour
⅓ cup water

Add noodles to large pan of boiling water, boil, uncovered, about 2 minutes or until tender; drain. Rinse under cold water; drain. Cool, then chop finely, place in bowl. Combine instant potato with boiling water in heatproof bowl. Add to noodles with onion, garlic, chicken, cheeses, egg and chives, mix well. Cover mixture, refrigerate 30 minutes.

Shape rounded tablespoons of mixture into croquettes. Toss croquettes in flour, shake away excess flour. Dip in combined extra eggs and milk, toss in bread crumbs. Repeat egg and crumbing process so croquettes are coated twice. Place onto tray, cover, refrigerate 30 minutes. Deep-fry croquettes in hot oil until golden brown and heated through; drain on absorbent paper. Serve with sauce.

Piquant Sauce: Heat butter in pan, add onions, cook, stirring, 1 minute. Stir in wine and vinegar, simmer about 5 minutes or until mixture is reduced by half. Add dill pickles, herbs and crumbled bouillon cube, simmer, uncovered, about 5 minutes or until reduced by about one-third. Blend flour with water in bowl, add to pan, stir over high heat until sauce boils and thickens.

Makes 24.

- Recipe can be prepared a day ahead; deep-fry just before serving. Sauce best made just before serving.
- Storage: Covered, in refrigerator.
- Freeze: Not suitable.
- Microwave: Not suitable.

CHICKEN QUENELLES WITH TARRAGON SAUCE

10oz boneless, skinless chicken
   breasts, chopped
2 egg whites
½ cup heavy cream
4 teaspoons chopped fresh tarragon
2 small chicken bouillon cubes
3 cups water

TARRAGON SAUCE
⅔ cup heavy cream
3 tablespoons brandy
3 tablespoons chopped fresh
   tarragon

Process chicken and egg whites until smooth. Transfer to bowl; fold in cream and tarragon.

Combine crumbled bouillon cubes and water in large pan. Bring to boil, reduce heat to simmer. Mold chicken mixture into oval shapes by using 2 wet dessert-spoons. Gently spoon mixture into simmering broth. Poach about 2 minutes on each side. Do not allow water to boil or quenelles will fall apart. Drain quenelles on absorbent paper. Serve with sauce.

Tarragon Sauce: Combine cream and brandy in pan, bring to boil, boil uncovered, until mixture is reduced by half; stir in tarragon.

Serves 4.

- Recipe is best made just before serving.
- Freeze: Not suitable.
- Microwave: Not suitable.

RIGHT: Clockwise from left: Chicken and Fresh Thyme Roulade; Chicken Croquettes with Piquant Sauce; Chicken Quenelles with Tarragon Sauce.

Cheese & Eggs

A sorbet to serve with cheese is one of the smart recipes in this section, plus some that could easily be adapted to serve as snacks, for lunch or a brunch. Most are at their delicious best served immediately after cooking, as eggs and cheese will toughen on reheating.

BASIL FRITTATA WITH PIMIENTO SAUCE

5 eggs
3 tablespoons milk
2 teaspoons all-purpose flour
½ cup grated Parmesan cheese
¼ cup chopped fresh basil
1 clove garlic, minced

PIMIENTO SAUCE
1 tablespoon butter
1 onion, thinly sliced
½ x 7oz can pimientos, sliced
¾ cup tomato puree
½ cup water
1 teaspoon sugar
½ teaspoon tabasco sauce

Whisk eggs, milk and flour together in large bowl, stir in remaining ingredients. Pour mixture into greased 8 inch ovenproof pie dish, bake in 350°F oven about 15 minutes or until just set. Stand a few minutes before cutting. Serve with pimiento sauce.

Pimiento Sauce: Melt butter in small pan, add onion, cook, stirring, until soft. Stir in remaining ingredients, simmer, uncovered, about 5 minutes or until mixture is slightly thickened.

Serves 4.

- Frittata best made just before serving. Sauce can be made a day ahead.
- Storage: Covered, in refrigerator.
- Freeze: Not suitable.
- Microwave: Sauce suitable.

CREAMY MUSHROOM SOUFFLE OMELETS

4 eggs, separated
4 teaspoons water
1 tablespoon butter

CREAMY MUSHROOM FILLING
2 tablespoons (¼ stick) butter
¼lb button mushrooms, sliced
4 teaspoons all-purpose flour
½ cup heavy cream
1 teaspoon fresh lemon juice
4 teaspoons chopped fresh chives

Whisk egg yolks and water together in bowl. Beat egg whites in bowl until soft peaks form, fold egg whites into yolk mixture in 2 batches. Preheat broiler to high. Heat butter in omelet pan, swirl evenly around pan. Spread half the mixture evenly into pan, cook over high heat about 20 seconds or until base begins to brown.

Broil omelet until top is set. Use spatula to slide omelet onto serving plate, spread half the filling over half the omelet; fold in half. Repeat with remaining omelet mixture and filling.

Creamy Mushroom Filling: Melt butter in pan, add mushrooms, cook, stirring, until tender. Stir in flour, cook, stirring, 1 minute. Remove from heat, gradually stir in cream and juice, stir over heat until mixture boils and thickens, stir in chives.

Serves 2.

- Omelets best made just before serving. If 2 pans are available it is easy to cook 2 omelets at the same time.
- Freeze: Not suitable.
- Microwave: Filling suitable.

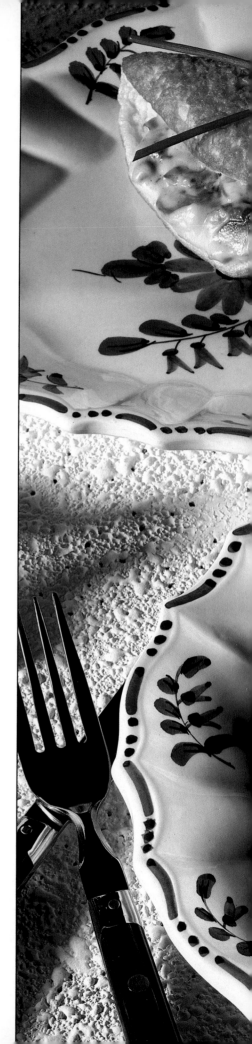

RIGHT: From top: Creamy Mushroom Souffle Omelets; Basil Frittata with Pimiento Sauce.

CHEESY PASTA MOLDS WITH SWEET CARROT SAUCE

1 small leek
3½oz vermicelli pasta
3 eggs, lightly beaten
½ cup sour cream
½ cup grated cheddar cheese
4 teaspoons grated Parmesan cheese
4 teaspoons chopped fresh parsley

SWEET CARROT SAUCE
2 carrots, chopped
2 cups water
4 teaspoons grated fresh gingerroot
4 teaspoons superfine sugar

Grease 4 ovenproof dishes (½ cup capacity). Remove 4 outer leaves from leek, cut into long strips about ½ inch wide. You will need 4 strips. Boil, steam or microwave leek strips until tender. Place 1 strip around inside of each dish.

Gradually add pasta to large pan of boiling water, boil, uncovered, until just tender, drain; cool. Combine eggs, cream, cheeses and parsley in bowl, stir in pasta; divide mixture between dishes. Cover each dish with lightly greased foil. Place in roasting pan, pour in enough boiling water to come halfway up sides of dishes. Bake in 350˚F oven about 30 minutes or until set. Remove from roasting pan, stand 5 minutes. Turn molds onto plates; spoon sauce around molds.

Sweet Carrot Sauce: Combine carrots, water, gingerroot and sugar in pan, stir over high heat until sugar is dissolved. Simmer, covered, about 10 minutes or until carrots are tender. Blend or process until sauce is smooth; strain; reheat before serving.

Serves 4.

■ Molds best made just before serving. Sauce can be made a day ahead.
■ Storage: Covered, in refrigerator.
■ Freeze: Sauce suitable.
■ Microwave: Sauce suitable.

EGGS WITH CUCUMBER CREAM DRESSING

4 eggs
1 small bunch watercress
cayenne pepper

CUCUMBER CREAM DRESSING
1 small green cucumber,
    finely chopped
¼ cup sour cream
⅓ cup heavy cream
1 small onion, finely chopped
4 teaspoons fresh lemon juice

Place eggs in pan, barely cover with cold water. Bring to boil, stirring gently to keep yolks centered; reduce heat, simmer 8 minutes. Remove from water, cover with cold water, gently break shells. Leave in cold water to cool completely. Shell eggs, cut in half lengthways, serve with watercress and dressing; sprinkle lightly with cayenne pepper.

Cucumber Cream Dressing: Place cucumber in sieve over bowl about 40 minutes to drain away excess liquid. Combine cucumber with remaining ingredients in bowl; mix well.

Serves 4.

■ Eggs best made just before serving. Dressing can be made several hours ahead.
■ Storage: Covered, in refrigerator.
■ Freeze: Not suitable.
■ Microwave: Not suitable.

RIGHT: Eggs with Cucumber Cream Dressing.
ABOVE: Cheesy Pasta Molds with Sweet Carrot Sauce.

PEAR AND ORANGE SALAD WITH CURRY DRESSING

We used harvati cheese in this recipe, gouda can be substituted.

2 pears
2 oranges
1 red onion, sliced
3½oz cheese, chopped
⅓ cup slivered almonds, toasted

CURRY DRESSING
½ cup light sour cream
½ teaspoon grated orange zest
¼ cup fresh orange juice
½ teaspoon curry powder
4 teaspoons chopped fresh parsley

Peel pears, slice thinly. Peel oranges thickly, cut into segments by cutting between membranes. Arrange pears, oranges, onion and cheese on serving plates, sprinkle with almonds. Top with dressing just before serving.
Curry Dressing: Combine cream, zest, juice and curry powder in bowl, whisk until combined; stir in parsley.

Serves 4.

- Salad best made just before serving.
- Freeze: Not suitable.

PEAR, GIN AND MINT SORBET

We served this sorbet with camembert cheese, sage derby cheese and herbed goats' milk cheese.

¾ cup water
¼ cup superfine sugar
1 teaspoon grated lemon zest
¼ cup fresh lemon juice
4 pears, peeled, chopped
¼ cup gin
3 tablespoons chopped fresh mint
1 egg white

Combine water, sugar, zest and juice in pan, stir over heat, without boiling, until sugar is dissolved. Add pears, simmer, uncovered, 3 minutes or until pears are tender. Remove from heat, add gin and mint; cool. Blend or process mixture until smooth, add egg white, blend until mixture is light. Pour into deep baking pan, cover with foil, freeze until firm. Scoop sorbet onto serving plates.

Serves 6.

- Sorbet can be made 3 days ahead.
- Storage: Covered, in freezer.
- Freeze: Suitable.
- Microwave: Not suitable.

RIGHT: From left: Pear, Gin and Mint Sorbet; Pear and Orange Salad with Curry Dressing.

FRIED CAMEMBERT WITH MANGO LIQUEUR SAUCE

15oz whole camembert cheese
all-purpose flour
2 eggs, lightly beaten
3 tablespoons milk
⅓ cup sesame seeds
1 cup packaged unseasoned
**   bread crumbs**
oil for deep-frying

MANGO LIQUEUR SAUCE
1 carrot, chopped
1 small onion, chopped
1 clove garlic, minced
1 small chicken bouillon cube
1 cup water
½ cup dry white wine
2 mangoes, chopped
4 teaspoons Grand Marnier

Cut camembert into 16 wedges; toss in flour, shake away excess flour. Dip wedges in combined eggs and milk, then in combined seeds and bread crumbs. Place wedges on tray, refrigerate 10 minutes. Dip wedges into egg mixture again, then seed mixture. Refrigerate further 10 minutes. Deep-fry in hot oil until golden brown; drain on absorbent paper.
Mango Liqueur Sauce: Combine carrot, onion, garlic, crumbled bouillon cube, water and wine in pan. Simmer, uncovered, about 10 minutes or until reduced by half; strain into bowl, return to clean pan. Blend, process or sieve mangoes until smooth. Add mango puree to pan with liqueur, reheat without boiling.
Makes 16.

- Cheese can be crumbed a day ahead; deep-fry just before serving.
- Storage: Covered, in refrigerator.
- Freeze: Not suitable.
- Microwave: Not suitable.

GOATS' MILK CHEESE TARTS

PASTRY
1¾ cups all-purpose flour
5oz (1¼ sticks) butter
1 egg yolk
2 teaspoons water, approximately
7oz goats' milk cheese,
**   finely chopped**
ground nutmeg

FILLING
1 tablespoon butter
8 green onions, finely chopped
3 eggs, lightly beaten
4 teaspoons seeded mustard
¼ cup fresh white bread crumbs
¾ cup heavy cream
¼ cup milk

Pastry: Sift flour into large bowl, rub in butter, stir in egg yolk and enough water to form a soft dough. Knead dough on lightly floured surface until smooth, cover; refrigerate 30 minutes. Divide pastry into 6 equal portions. Roll portions on lightly floured surface or between pieces of paper until large enough to line 6 x 4 inch flan pans (with removeable bases). Lift pastry into pans, trim edges; stand pans on baking sheet. Cover pastry cases with paper, fill with dried beans or rice. Bake in 375˚F oven 7 minutes, remove paper and beans, bake further 7 minutes.

Divide cheese between cases, pour filling over cheese, sprinkle lightly with nutmeg. Bake in 350˚F oven about 25 minutes or until set and lightly browned. Stand tarts 5 minutes before serving.
Filling: Melt butter in pan, add onions, cook, stirring, until soft. Combine onions, eggs, mustard, bread crumbs, cream and milk in bowl.

Makes 6.

- Pastry cases can be made a week ahead.
- Storage: In airtight container.
- Freeze: Not suitable.
- Microwave: Not suitable.

RIGHT: Goats' Milk Cheese Tarts.
ABOVE: Fried Camembert with Mango Liqueur Sauce.

CRISPY CHEESE CREPES WITH TOMATO ONION SAUCE

all-purpose flour
1 egg, lightly beaten
4 teaspoons water
½ cup packaged unseasoned
    bread crumbs
oil for deep-frying

CREPES
½ cup all-purpose flour
2 eggs
4 teaspoons light olive oil
¾ cup milk

CHEESE FILLING
¼ cup (½ stick) butter
⅓ cup all-purpose flour
1 cup milk
7oz Gruyere cheese, grated
2 egg yolks

TOMATO ONION SAUCE
2 tomatoes, peeled, seeded
4 teaspoons olive oil
1 small onion, finely chopped
4 teaspoons tomato paste
3 tablespoons water

Place 2 crepes together, just slightly over-lapping, spread with one-third warm cheese filling. Roll up from shortest side like a jelly-roll. Repeat with remaining crepes and filling. Wrap rolls tightly in baking paper, twist ends firmly to hold in shape; refrigerate 1 hour or until firm. Un-wrap rolls, trim and discard ends.

Cut each roll into 6 slices, toss in flour, shake away excess flour, dip in combined egg and water, then in bread crumbs. Refrigerate 15 minutes. Deep-fry slices in batches in hot oil until golden brown; drain on absorbent paper. Serve with sauce.

Crepes: Sift flour into bowl, gradually stir in combined eggs, oil and milk, mix to a smooth batter (or blend or process all ingredients until smooth). Cover, stand 30 minutes. Pour 3 to 4 tablespoons of batter into heated greased 9½ inch crepe pan; cook until lightly browned underneath. Turn crepe, brown on other side. Repeat with remaining batter. You will need 6 crepes for this recipe.

Cheese Filling: Melt butter in pan, stir in flour, cook, stirring, 1 minute. Remove from heat, gradually stir in milk, stir over high heat until mixture boils and thickens. Remove from heat, add cheese, stir until melted. Stir in egg yolks, cool slightly before using.

Tomato Onion Sauce: Chop tomatoes finely. Heat oil in pan, add onion, cook, stirring, until soft. Add tomatoes, paste and water, simmer 5 minutes.

Serves 6.

■ Uncrumbed crepes can be made 2 days ahead. Crumb and deep-fry just before serving. Sauce can be made 2 days ahead.
■ Storage: Covered, in refrigerator.
■ Freeze: Unfilled crepes suitable.
■ Microwave: Sauce suitable.

QUAIL EGG AND PESTO TARTS

1 cup all-purpose flour
3oz (¾ stick) butter, chopped
1 egg yolk
1 teaspoon fresh lemon juice
18 quail eggs

PESTO MAYONNAISE
4 teaspoons mayonnaise
3 tablespoons sour cream
1 tablespoon chopped fresh basil
1 tablespoon grated Parmesan
    cheese
2 teaspoons fresh lemon juice
1 clove garlic, minced
1 teaspoon water

Lightly grease 12 boat-shaped tart tins (2 inches x 4½ inches). Sift flour into bowl, rub in butter, stir in combined egg yolk and juice, mix to a soft dough. Turn dough onto lightly floured surface, knead until smooth, cover, refrigerate 15 minutes.

Roll pastry out thinly on lightly floured surface (or between plastic wrap or baking paper). Cut out boat shapes, press gently into tart tins. Prick pastry cases all over, bake in 375°F oven about 10 minutes or until lightly browned. Remove from tins to wire rack; cool.

Place eggs in pan, barely cover with cold water, bring to boil, stirring gently so yolks will be centered. Reduce heat, simmer 4 minutes, place in cold water to cool completely. Shell eggs, cut in half lengthways. Place 3 halves in each pastry case, top with pesto mayonnaise.

Pesto Mayonnaise: Combine all ingredients in bowl.

Makes 12.

■ Pastry cases can be made 3 days ahead.
■ Storage: In airtight container.
■ Freeze: Pastry cases suitable.
■ Microwave: Not suitable.

RIGHT: Quail Egg and Pesto Tarts.
LEFT: Crispy Cheese Crepes with Tomato Onion Sauce.

RICOTTA ROLL WITH TOMATO VINAIGRETTE

½lb ricotta cheese
8oz package cream cheese, softened
¼ cup grated Parmesan cheese
2 tablespoons chopped fresh basil
1 clove garlic, minced
1 teaspoon sambal oelek
1 slice bacon, finely chopped
3½ teaspoons unflavored gelatin
3 tablespoons water
18 stuffed green olives
½ bunch (10oz) spinach

TOMATO VINAIGRETTE
2 tomatoes, peeled, seeded
½ small onion, finely chopped
½ cup olive oil
⅓ cup white vinegar
1 teaspoon chopped fresh basil
1 teaspoon sugar
1 teaspoon Worcestershire sauce

Beat ricotta and cream cheese in bowl with electric mixer until smooth, stir in Parmesan, basil, garlic and sambal oelek. Cook bacon in skillet until crisp; drain on absorbent paper.

Sprinkle gelatin over water in cup, stand in small pan of simmering water, stir until dissolved. Cool to room temperature; do not allow to set. Add bacon, gelatin mixture and olives to cheese mixture; mix well.

Boil, steam or microwave spinach until wilted, rinse under cold water, pat dry with absorbent paper. Lay spinach leaves in single layer, slightly overlapping, on sheet of plastic wrap, forming 6 inch x 12 inch rectangle. Spoon cheese mixture on long side of spinach, leaving 2 inch border. Fold ends of spinach in, roll up like a jelly-roll, using plastic to lift and guide roll. Wrap securely in foil; refrigerate several hours or overnight. Serve sliced with vinaigrette.

Tomato Vinaigrette: Chop tomatoes finely, combine in small bowl with remaining ingredients.

Serves 8.

■ Roll can be made 3 days ahead.
■ Storage: Covered, in refrigerator.
■ Freeze: Not suitable.
■ Microwave: Suitable.

LEFT: Ricotta Roll with Tomato Vinaigrette.

CAULIFLOWER, BACON AND CHEESE SOUFFLES

4 teaspoons packaged unseasoned bread crumbs
7oz cauliflower
1 tablespoon butter
1 small onion, chopped
2 slices bacon, finely chopped
2 tablespoons (1/4 stick) butter, extra
4 teaspoons all-purpose flour
1/3 cup milk
2 eggs, separated
3 tablespoons grated cheddar cheese
4 teaspoons grated Parmesan cheese
2 teaspoons grated Parmesan cheese, extra
2 teaspoons grated cheddar cheese, extra

Grease 4 souffle dishes (1/2 cup capacity), sprinkle with bread crumbs, place on baking sheet. Boil, steam or microwave cauliflower until tender; drain. Blend or process until smooth. Melt butter in pan, add onion and bacon, cook, stirring, until onion is soft; drain.

Melt extra butter in pan, stir in flour, cook, stirring, 1 minute. Remove from heat, gradually stir in milk. Stir over high heat until mixture boils and thickens; cool mixture slightly.

Stir in egg yolks, cheeses, cauliflower and onion mixture. Beat egg whites in small bowl until firm peaks form, fold through cauliflower mixture. Pour into prepared dishes, sprinkle with combined extra cheeses, bake in 375°F oven 20 minutes, or until puffed and browned.

Serves 4.

- Make souffles just before serving.
- Freeze: Not suitable.
- Microwave: Not suitable.

ONION CHEESE TARTS

PASTRY
3/4 cup whole-wheat flour
1/4 cup (1/2 stick) butter
3 tablespoons water, approximately
1/4 cup grated cheddar cheese

ONION CHEESE FILLING
1 tablespoon butter
1 large onion, thinly sliced
2 eggs, lightly beaten
3 tablespoons sour cream
1/2 cup grated cheddar cheese
4 teaspoons chopped fresh parsley

Pastry: Grease 12 boat-shaped tart tins (2 inches x 4 1/2 inches). Sift flour into large bowl, rub in butter, add enough water to mix to a soft dough. Knead gently on lightly floured surface until smooth; cover, refrigerate 30 minutes. Roll dough out thinly on lightly floured surface, cut out 12 boat shapes, press into tins, trim edges.

Prick all over with fork, cover, refrigerate 20 minutes. Bake in 375°F oven 10 minutes; remove from oven. Place 1 rounded tablespoon of onion filling into each pastry case. Sprinkle with cheese. Bake in 350°F oven about 15 minutes or until lightly browned. Remove from tins to wire rack to cool.

Onion Cheese Filling: Melt butter in pan, add onion, cook, stirring, until soft; drain on absorbent paper. Whisk eggs and sour cream together in bowl, stir in cheese, parsley and onion mixture.

Makes 12.

- Pastry can be prepared a day ahead. Tarts are best made just before serving.
- Storage: Covered, in refrigerator.
- Freeze: Not suitable.
- Microwave: Not suitable.

EGGS FLORENTINE

6 large spinach leaves, shredded
1 tablespoon butter
2 English muffins
2 teaspoons butter, extra
2 teaspoons seeded mustard
4 slices cooked ham
4 eggs
paprika

CHEESE SAUCE
2 teaspoons butter
2 teaspoons all-purpose flour
2/3 cup milk
1/2 cup grated cheddar cheese
1 tablespoon butter, extra

Boil, steam or microwave spinach until wilted, drain; add butter, keep warm.

Toast split muffins, spread with combined extra butter and mustard. Top muffin halves with ham and spinach. Poach eggs in simmering water until done as desired. Place eggs on spinach, top with hot sauce, sprinkle with paprika.

Cheese Sauce: Melt butter in pan, stir in flour, cook, stirring, 1 minute. Remove from heat, gradually stir in milk, stir over high heat until mixture boils and thickens. Add cheese and extra butter, stir until cheese is melted.

Serves 4.

- Recipe best made just before serving.
- Freeze: Not suitable.
- Microwave: Suitable.

RIGHT: Eggs Florentine.
BELOW: From left: Onion Cheese Tarts; Cauliflower, Bacon and Cheese Souffles.

Appetizers

Meat

Crepes, pasta, pancakes and pastry parcels are among the smart and tempting appetizers here, as is meat teamed wonderfully with fruit. For the more adventurous we have included frogs' legs in luscious garlic sauce. Some of the heartier recipes would also be delicious mini meals.

LEMON CREPES WITH LAMB AND MINTED YOGURT

LEMON CREPES
½ cup all-purpose flour
2 eggs, lightly beaten
4 teaspoons light olive oil
¾ cup milk
1 teaspoon grated lemon zest

LAMB FILLING
1 tablespoon butter
1 small onion, finely chopped
1 clove garlic, minced
3½oz button mushrooms,
    finely chopped
1 teaspoon grated fresh gingerroot
½lb ground lamb
1 teaspoon ground cumin
½ teaspoon garam masala
3 tablespoons tomato ketchup
4 teaspoons chopped fresh cilantro
½ cup fresh bread crumbs
½ cup plain yogurt

MINTED YOGURT
¾ cup plain yogurt
4 teaspoons fresh lemon juice
3 tablespoons chopped fresh mint
1 teaspoon superfine sugar

Lemon Crepes: Sift flour into bowl, gradually stir in combined eggs, oil and milk, mix to a smooth batter (or blend or process all ingredients until smooth). Cover, stand 30 minutes, stir in zest. Pour 3 tablespoons of batter into heated greased crepe pan; cook until lightly browned underneath. Turn crepe, brown on other side. Repeat with remaining batter. You will need 12 crepes for this recipe.

Spread each crepe evenly with filling, fold crepes into parcels. Place crepes in single layer in ovenproof dish, cover, bake in 350°F oven about 15 minutes or until heated through. Serve with minted yogurt.
Lamb Filling: Heat butter in pan, add onion, garlic and mushrooms, cover, cook about 2 minutes or until onion is soft. Stir in gingerroot, lamb, cumin, garam masala, ketchup, cilantro and bread crumbs. Cover, simmer about 15 minutes or until lamb is tender, stirring occasionally. Add yogurt, stir until heated through.
Minted Yogurt: Combine all ingredients in small bowl.

Serves 4.

- Filling and yogurt can be made a day ahead. Crepes can be made 2 days ahead.
- Storage: Filling and yogurt, covered, in refrigerator. Crepes, layered with paper, in refrigerator.
- Freeze: Crepes suitable.
- Microwave: Filling suitable.

RIGHT: From top: Cornmeal Crepes with Avocado Cream; Lemon Crepes with Lamb and Minted Yogurt.

CORNMEAL CREPES WITH AVOCADO CREAM

CORNMEAL CREPES
1/4 cup all-purpose flour
3 tablespoons cornmeal
2/3 cup milk
1 egg, lightly beaten
1 tablespoon butter, melted
1/4 cup tomato puree
1/3 cup coarsely grated Parmesan cheese

FILLING
4 teaspoons olive oil
1 clove garlic, minced
1 onion, finely chopped
7oz ground beef
8 3/4oz can red kidney beans, drained, mashed
3/4 cup tomato puree
1/2 teaspoon tabasco sauce
1 small beef bouillon cube

AVOCADO CREAM
1/2 avocado, chopped
2 teaspoons fresh lemon juice
4 teaspoons light sour cream

Cornmeal Crepes: Sift flour into bowl, add cornmeal, gradually stir in combined milk, egg and butter, mix until well combined (or blend or process all ingredients). Cover, stand 30 minutes. Pour 3 tablespoons of batter into heated greased crepe pan; cook until lightly browned underneath. Turn crepe, brown on other side. Repeat with remaining batter. You will need 6 crepes for this recipe.

Spread each crepe evenly with filling, fold into quarters. Place filled crepes into greased shallow ovenproof dish, spread with tomato puree, sprinkle with cheese. Bake in 350°F oven about 15 minutes or until cheese is melted. Serve with avocado cream.

Filling: Heat oil in pan, add garlic and onion, cook, stirring, until onion is soft. Add beef, cook, stirring, until browned. Stir in beans, puree, sauce and crumbled bouillon cube, simmer, uncovered, about 10 minutes or until thick. Cool 5 minutes before using.

Avocado Cream: Blend or process all ingredients until smooth.

Serves 6.

■ Filling for crepes can be made a day ahead. Unfilled crepes can be made 2 days ahead.
■ Storage: Filling, covered, in refrigerator. Crepes, layered with paper, in refrigerator.
■ Freeze: Unfilled crepes and filling suitable.
■ Microwave: Filling suitable.

SPICY PORK AND RICE BALLS

2 tablespoons (¼ stick) butter, melted
1 clove garlic, minced
1½ cups short-grain rice
¼ cup dry white wine
3 cups water
1 small chicken bouillon cube
1 cup coarsely grated Parmesan
    cheese
2 eggs, lightly beaten
all-purpose flour
1 egg, extra
4 teaspoons water, extra
¼ cup packaged unseasoned
    bread crumbs
oil for deep-frying

SPICY PORK FILLING
5oz barbequed pork, finely chopped
2 green onions, chopped
2 teaspoons oyster-flavored sauce
2 teaspoons hoisin sauce
2 teaspoons water
1 teaspoon sambal oelek

Melt butter in pan, add garlic and rice, cook, stirring, until rice is coated with butter. Add wine, water and crumbled bouillon cube, simmer, covered, over low heat about 15 minutes or until almost all the liquid is absorbed. Remove from heat, quickly stir in cheese and eggs. Spread mixture into greased 8 inch x 12 inch baking pan, cover, refrigerate until firm. Divide rice mixture evenly into 16 portions.

Divide each portion in half, place one half in palm of hand, form a hollow, fill with a heaped teaspoon of filling. Cover with remaining half portion of rice, shape into a ball. Repeat with remaining rice mixture and filling. Place rice balls onto tray; refrigerate 15 minutes.

Toss balls in flour, shake away excess flour, dip into combined extra egg and extra water, then in bread crumbs. Deep-fry rice balls in batches in hot oil until golden brown; drain on absorbent paper.
Spicy Pork Filling: Combine all ingredients in bowl.

Makes 16.

- Recipe can be prepared 2 days ahead; deep-fry just before serving.
- Storage: Covered, in refrigerator.
- Freeze: Suitable.
- Microwave: Not suitable.

PEARS AND PROSCIUTTO WITH FIG GINGERROOT COMPOTE

3 pears
6 slices prosciutto

FIG GINGERROOT COMPOTE
½ cup dark brown sugar
3 tablespoons white wine vinegar
1 cup water
½ teaspoon grated lemon zest
2 teaspoons fresh lemon juice
1 cinnamon stick
½ teaspoon ground gingerroot
2 tablespoons chopped glace
    gingerroot
½ cup quartered dried figs

Peel pears, cut in half lengthways, remove core, slice pears as pictured. Place half a pear on each plate, serve with prosciutto and compote.
Fig Gingerroot Compote: Combine sugar, vinegar and water in pan, stir over heat, without boiling, until sugar is dissolved. Add remaining ingredients, simmer, uncovered, about 40 minutes or until figs are soft.

Cool compote to room temperature or refrigerate before serving.

Serves 6.

- Compote can be made a week ahead.
- Storage: Covered, in refrigerator.
- Freeze: Not suitable.
- Microwave: Not suitable.

BELOW: Spicy Pork and Rice Balls.
RIGHT: Pears and Prosciutto with Fig Gingerroot Compote.

until heated through. Serve kidneys and madeira sauce on crispy croutes.

Crispy Croutes: Cut each bread slice into heart shape. Shallow-fry in hot oil until golden brown; drain on absorbent paper. Coat half of each heart with parsley.

Serves 6.

- ■ Recipe best made just before serving.
- ■ Freeze: Not suitable.
- ■ Microwave: Not suitable.

CRUMBED BRAINS WITH MUSHROOM BUTTER SAUCE

4 sets lambs' brains
all-purpose flour
1 egg, lightly beaten
3 tablespoons milk
1½ cups fresh bread crumbs
oil for deep-frying

MUSHROOM BUTTER SAUCE
½ cup (1 stick) butter
2 cloves garlic, minced
4 green onions, finely chopped
½lb button mushrooms, sliced
3 tablespoons chopped fresh chives
3 tablespoons chopped fresh parsley
4 teaspoons fresh lemon juice

Place brains in bowl, cover with cold water, stand 1 hour, drain, peel away membrane. Place brains in pan, cover with cold water, simmer, uncovered, about 2 minutes or until just cooked. Drain on absorbent paper; cool to room temperature.

Dust brains lightly with flour, shake away excess flour, dip into combined egg and milk, toss in bread crumbs. Deep-fry brains in hot oil until golden brown; drain on absorbent paper. Serve brains with mushroom butter sauce.

Mushroom Butter Sauce: Heat butter in pan, add garlic, onions and mushrooms, cover, cook over low heat about 10 minutes or until mushrooms are soft. Stir in chives, parsley and juice.

Serves 4.

- ■ Brains can be crumbed several hours ahead. Sauce best made just before serving.
- ■ Storage: Covered, in refrigerator.
- ■ Freeze: Not suitable.
- ■ Microwave: Not suitable.

MUSTARD CREPE WHIRLS WITH PORK AND TAMARIND

MUSTARD CREPES
¾ cup all-purpose flour
2 eggs, lightly beaten
4 teaspoons light olive oil
1 teaspoon French mustard
1 cup milk
¾lb barbequed pork, sliced

TAMARIND SAUCE
3 tablespoons teriyaki sauce
2 teaspoons tamarind sauce
1 teaspoon drained green peppercorns, crushed
1 clove garlic, minced
½ teaspoon five-spice powder

Mustard Crepes: Sift flour into bowl, gradually stir in combined eggs, oil, mustard and milk. Mix to a smooth batter (or blend or process all ingredients until smooth). Cover, stand 30 minutes. Pour 3 to 4 tablespoons of batter into heated greased crepe pan; cook until lightly browned underneath. Turn crepe, brown on other side. Repeat with remaining batter. You will need 8 crepes for this recipe.

Roll crepes tightly, slice evenly. Place crepes on serving plate, top with pork and tamarind sauce.

Tamarind Sauce: Combine all ingredients in bowl.

Serves 6 to 8.

- ■ Crepes can be made 2 days ahead. Sauce is best made just before serving.
- ■ Storage: Crepes, layered with paper, in refrigerator.
- ■ Freeze: Crepes suitable.
- ■ Microwave: Not suitable.

KIDNEYS ON CRISPY CROUTES WITH MADEIRA SAUCE

6 lambs' kidneys
3oz (¾ stick) butter
8 pearl onions, sliced
4 teaspoons all-purpose flour
4 teaspoons madeira
1 cup water
1 large chicken bouillon cube
4 teaspoons tomato paste

CRISPY CROUTES
6 slices white bread
oil for shallow-frying
3 tablespoons chopped fresh parsley

Remove membrane from kidneys, slice kidneys in half lengthways, remove cores. Heat butter in skillet, add kidneys, cook over low heat about 5 minutes or until just cooked; remove from skillet. Add onions to skillet, cook, stirring, until soft. Stir in flour, cook, stirring, 1 minute. Remove from heat, stir in combined madeira, water, crumbled bouillon cube and paste, stir over heat until mixture boils and thickens. Add kidneys, cook, without boiling,

RIGHT: From top: Kidneys on Crispy Croutes with Madeira Sauce; Crumbed Brains with Mushroom Butter Sauce. ABOVE LEFT: Mustard Crepe Whirls with Pork and Tamarind.

PEPPERONI, ZUCCHINI AND PASTA SALAD

2½ cups (7oz) pasta
2 zucchini
¼lb pepperoni salami, sliced

DRESSING
¼ cup olive oil
⅓ cup red wine vinegar
3 tablespoons fresh lemon juice
6 pitted black olives, finely chopped
2 teaspoons superfine sugar
4 teaspoons chopped fresh basil
1 small fresh red chili, finely chopped
1 clove garlic, minced

Gradually add pasta to large pan of boiling water, boil, uncovered, about 10 minutes or until just tender; drain. Rinse under cold water; drain. Boil, steam or microwave zucchini until just tender; drain, cool, slice finely. Combine pasta, zucchini, salami and dressing in bowl.

Dressing: Combine ingredients in bowl.
Serves 4.

- ■ Salad can be made a day ahead.
- ■ Freeze: Not suitable.
- ■ Microwave: Suitable.

FRIED RAVIOLI WITH GREEN PEPPERCORN SAUCE

½lb ravioli
all-purpose flour
4 teaspoons milk
1 egg, lightly beaten
1 cup fresh bread crumbs
oil for deep-frying

GREEN PEPPERCORN SAUCE
1 tablespoon butter
**2 teaspoons drained green
  peppercorns, crushed**
1 egg yolk
½ cup heavy cream
4 teaspoons marsala

Dust ravioli lightly with flour, shake away excess flour. Dip ravioli in combined milk and egg, then coat in bread crumbs. Deep-fry in batches in hot oil until golden brown; drain on absorbent paper. Serve with green peppercorn sauce.

Green Peppercorn Sauce: Melt butter with peppercorns in pan. Stir in combined egg yolk, cream and marsala, stir over heat, without boiling, until sauce thickens slightly; serve immediately.

Serves 4.

- ■ Ravioli can be crumbed several hours ahead; deep-fry just before serving.
- ■ Storage: Covered, in refrigerator.
- ■ Freeze: Not suitable.
- ■ Microwave: Not suitable.

TORTELLINI WITH SUN-DRIED TOMATOES

2 tablespoons (¼ stick) butter
1 small onion, chopped
1 clove garlic, minced
½ cup drained sun-dried tomatoes
3 tablespoons tomato paste
1 small fresh red chili
**   pepper, chopped**
½ teaspoon sugar
2½oz salami, chopped
½lb tortellini
4 teaspoons chopped fresh parsley

Melt butter in pan, add onion and garlic, cook, stirring, until onion is soft. Process onion mixture, tomatoes, paste, chili pepper and sugar to a paste. Transfer mixture to pan, add salami, stir over low heat until heated through; keep warm.

Add tortellini to large pan of boiling water, boil, uncovered, about 10 minutes or until tender; drain. Return tortellini to pan, add tomato mixture, stir over low heat until heated through, serve sprinkled with parsley.

Serves 6.

▨ Tomato mixture can be prepared a day ahead. Tortellini best cooked just before serving.
▨ Storage: Covered, in refrigerator.
▨ Freeze: Not suitable.
▨ Microwave: Suitable.

ABOVE: Pepperoni, Zucchini and Pasta Salad.
LEFT: From top: Tortellini with Sun-Dried Tomatoes; Fried Ravioli with Green Peppercorn Sauce.

HAM AND TWO CHEESE SALAD

¼lb gruyere cheese
¼lb cooked ham
1 small red bell pepper
1½ cups finely shredded cabbage
1 cup watercress sprigs
4 romaine lettuce leaves

ROQUEFORT DRESSING
¼ cup red wine vinegar
1 clove garlic, minced
1 teaspoon seeded mustard
⅓ cup salad oil
1oz Roquefort cheese, crumbled

Cut cheese, cooked ham and pepper into thin strips, combine in large bowl with cabbage and watercress; toss gently. Serve on lettuce leaves. Top with dressing just before serving.
Roquefort Dressing: Combine all ingredients in bowl.

Serves 4.

- Recipe best made just before serving.
- Freeze: Not suitable.

FROGS' LEGS IN GARLIC CREAM SAUCE

12 pairs frogs' legs
all-purpose flour
2 tablespoons (¼ stick) butter
4 teaspoons olive oil
2 cloves garlic, minced
3 tablespoons dry white wine
1¼ cups heavy cream
¼ cup milk
2 teaspoons fresh lemon juice
3 tablespoons chopped fresh parsley

Remove top flap from each pair of legs. Cut through center of legs to separate. Dust legs lightly with flour, shake away excess flour. Heat butter and oil in skillet, add garlic and legs, cook over low heat until cooked through. Remove from heat, keep warm. Add wine, cream, milk and juice to skillet, bring to boil, reduce heat. Stir over medium heat, without boiling, until sauce is thickened slightly; stir in parsley just before serving.

Serves 6.

- Recipe best made just before serving.
- Freeze: Not suitable.
- Microwave: Not suitable.

ABOVE: Ham and Two Cheese Salad.
RIGHT: Frogs' Legs in Garlic Cream Sauce.

BROWN RICE PANCAKES WITH ROAST BEEF

½ cup self-rising flour
½ cup cooked brown rice
2 eggs, lightly beaten
3 tablespoons milk
¼ cup (½ stick) butter
cracked black pepper
10oz beef tenderloin
3 tablespoons olive oil
4 teaspoons all-purpose flour
½ cup dry red wine
1 small beef bouillon cube
1 cup water
2 tablespoons (¼ stick) butter, extra
2 teaspoons French mustard

Sift flour into bowl, gradually stir in combined rice, eggs and milk. Melt butter in skillet, drop heaped tablespoons of rice mixture into skillet, flatten slightly, cook 2 minutes on each side; keep warm. You will need 8 pancakes for this recipe. Sprinkle pepper evenly over beef. Heat oil in skillet, add beef, cook about 3 minutes on each side or until cooked as desired. Stand 5 minutes before slicing beef thinly.

Pour excess oil from skillet, leaving 4 teaspoons in skillet. Add flour, cook, stirring, until lightly browned. Remove from heat, gradually stir in combined wine, crumbled bouillon cube and water, stir over high heat until mixture boils and thickens. Whisk in extra butter and mustard. Serve brown rice pancakes with the beef and sauce.

Serves 4.

■ Beef and sauce best made just before serving. Rice pancakes can be made 2 days ahead.
■ Storage: Layered with paper, in refrigerator.
■ Freeze: Pancakes suitable.
■ Microwave: Not suitable.

LAMB AND WALNUT PARCELS WITH HONEY AND ROSEMARY

3 small lamb fillets
2 tablespoons (¼ stick) butter
1 clove garlic, minced
3 sheets phyllo pastry
¼ cup (½ stick) butter, melted, extra
1 cup walnut pieces, finely chopped

HONEY ROSEMARY GLAZE
1 teaspoon cornstarch
⅓ cup water
3 tablespoons honey
1 tablespoon butter
4 teaspoons chopped fresh rosemary

Cut fillets in half crossways. Melt butter in skillet, add lamb and garlic, cook over high heat until lamb is browned all over; cool to room temperature. Brush each sheet of pastry with extra butter, sprinkle evenly with walnuts. Cut each sheet in half crossways, place a piece of lamb on edge of long side of pastry, fold edges of pastry in, roll up. Place parcels on greased baking sheet, brush with remaining butter, bake in 375°F oven about 20 minutes or until browned. Serve with hot glaze.

Honey Rosemary Glaze: Blend cornstarch with water in pan, add honey, butter and rosemary, stir over high heat until mixture boils and thickens.

Serves 6.

■ Parcels and glaze can be prepared several hours ahead; cook just before serving.
■ Storage: Covered, in refrigerator.
■ Freeze: Not suitable.
■ Microwave: Not suitable.

ABOVE: Lamb and Walnut Parcels with Honey and Rosemary.
LEFT: Brown Rice Pancakes with Roast Beef.

Soups

Seafood

The refined flavors of seafood are very popular in soups ranging from light consommes to heartier chowders. Remember to be careful when cooking any seafood because it toughens easily with overcooking or reheating.

MUSSEL CHOWDER

20 mussels
1 tablespoon butter
2 slices bacon, finely chopped
1 red bell pepper, finely chopped
1 small onion, finely chopped
3 tablespoons all-purpose flour
1½ cups milk
1 cup water
1 small potato, finely chopped
3 green onions, finely chopped

Remove beards from mussels, scrub shells. Add mussels to large pan of boiling water, simmer, covered, about 2 minutes or until shells have opened. Remove mussel meat from shells.

Heat butter in pan, add bacon, pepper and onion, cook, stirring, until pepper is soft.

Add flour, cook, stirring, 1 minute. Remove from heat, gradually stir in milk and water, add potato, stir over high heat until mixture boils and thickens. Reduce heat, simmer few minutes until potato is cooked, add mussels and green onions, reheat mixture without boiling.

Serves 4.

▪ Chowder best made just before serving.
▪ Freeze: Not suitable.
▪ Microwave: Suitable.

FISH SOUP WITH TOMATOES AND OREGANO

¾lb white fish cutlets
3 tablespoons light olive oil
1 onion, chopped
1 clove garlic, minced
½ cup dry white wine
14½oz can tomatoes
4 teaspoons tomato paste
3 cups water
2 teaspoons chopped fresh oregano
2 teaspoons superfine sugar

Remove skin and bones from fish, cut fish into pieces. Heat oil in large pan, add onion and garlic, cook, stirring, until onion is soft; stir in wine. Simmer, uncovered, about 3 minutes or until liquid is reduced by half. Add undrained crushed tomatoes, paste, water and oregano. Simmer, covered, 20 minutes. Add fish and sugar, simmer, covered, about 2 minutes or until fish is just cooked.

Serves 4.

▪ Recipe best made just before serving.
▪ Freeze: Not suitable.
▪ Microwave: Suitable.

SEAFOOD AND FRESH VEGETABLE CONSOMME

12 cups water
2 carrots, chopped
2 leeks, chopped
2 stalks celery, chopped
1 onion, chopped
2 large tomatoes, chopped
1lb mussels
4 uncooked jumbo shrimp, shelled
8 sea scallops
½ cup dry white wine
½ cup water, extra
3 green onions, chopped
2 teaspoons thinly sliced fresh gingerroot
1 small clove garlic, minced
7oz broccoli, chopped
4 teaspoons tomato puree
1 carrot, sliced, extra
1 stalk celery, sliced, extra
4 green onions, chopped, extra

Combine water, carrots, leeks, celery, onion and tomatoes in large pan, simmer, uncovered, about 1 hour or until liquid is reduced by half.

Strain through fine cloth, discard vegetables (you should have about 6 cups broth).

Remove beards from mussels, scrub shells. Slice shrimp lengthways. Remove coral from scallops, cut scallops into quarters. Combine wine, extra water, green onions, gingerroot and garlic in pan, bring to boil, reduce heat. Add mussels, cook about 2 minutes or until mussels open, remove from pan. Add shrimp, scallops and scallop coral to pan, cook about 30 seconds or until seafood is just cooked.

Combine vegetable broth, broccoli, tomato puree, extra carrot and extra celery in large pan, simmer, covered, about 5 minutes or until extra carrot and celery are tender. Add all seafood with liquid and extra green onions, stir until soup is heated through.

Serves 8.

▪ Broth can be made a day ahead. Soup best made just before serving.
▪ Storage: Covered, in refrigerator.
▪ Freeze: Broth suitable.
▪ Microwave: Not suitable.

RIGHT: Clockwise from left: Fish Soup with Tomatoes and Oregano; Mussel Chowder; Seafood and Fresh Vegetable Consomme.

SPICY CREAMED SHRIMP SOUP

½lb cooked shrimp
5 cups water
3 tablespoons butter
1 onion, chopped
1 carrot, chopped
1 clove garlic, minced
¼ teaspoon dried basil leaves
¼ teaspoon dried thyme leaves
1 large chicken bouillon cube
3 tablespoons tomato paste
3 tablespoons dry sherry
⅓ cup all-purpose flour
⅓ cup water, extra
1¼ cups heavy cream

Shell and devein shrimp, place shells and heads in pan with the water, simmer, uncovered, 20 minutes; strain broth.

Chop shrimp finely. Heat butter in large pan, add onion, carrot and garlic, cook, stirring, until onion is soft. Add shrimp broth, basil, thyme, crumbled bouillon cube, paste and sherry. Simmer, uncovered, 5 minutes. Blend or process mixture in several batches until smooth. Return to pan, stir in blended flour and extra water. Stir over high heat until soup boils and thickens. Remove from heat, stir in cream and half the shrimp, reheat without boiling.

Serve soup sprinkled with remaining chopped shrimp.

Serves 6.

- Soup can be made a day ahead.
- Storage: Covered, in refrigerator.
- Freeze: Not suitable.
- Microwave: Not suitable.

SCALLOP AND SWEET POTATO SOUP

3 tablespoons light olive oil
1 onion, chopped
1lb sweet white potato, chopped
2½ cups water
1 large vegetable bouillon cube
15oz sea scallops
1¼ cups milk
2 egg yolks
½ cup heavy cream
2 tablespoons chopped fresh chives
1in piece fresh gingerroot chopped
8 shucked oysters

Heat oil in pan, add onion, cook, stirring, until soft. Add potato, cover tightly, cook over low heat 15 minutes. Combine water and crumbled bouillon cube.

Blend or process potato mixture with ¼ cup of the bouillon cube mixture. Return to pan with remaining bouillon cube mixture, simmer 15 minutes. Reserve coral from scallops, chop white part, place white part in pan with milk. Bring to boil, drain immediately, discard milk. Stir in scallops, reserved coral, egg yolks, cream, chives, gingerroot and oysters. Reheat soup without boiling.

Serves 4.

- Soup best made just before serving.
- Freeze: Not suitable.
- Microwave: Not suitable.

ABOVE: From top: Spicy Creamed Shrimp Soup; Scallop and Sweet Potato Soup.

Soups

Vegetable

Possibly the most popular soups are based on vegetables and there are clear, cream, thick, smooth and chunky soups in this section. Some recipes are surprisingly simple, all will be fresh taste experiences.

DOUBLE POTATO SOUP

2 tablespoons (¼ stick) butter
2 large (14oz) potatoes, chopped
1 onion, sliced
1 bay leaf
1½ cups water
½ large chicken bouillon cube
¼ cup heavy cream
3 tablespoons chopped fresh chives

SWEET POTATO SOUP
2 tablespoons (¼ stick) butter
14oz sweet potato, chopped
1¾ cups water
½ large chicken bouillon cube
3 tablespoons heavy cream

Melt butter in pan, add potatoes, onion and bay leaf, cover, cook over medium heat until onion is soft. Stir in water, crumbled bouillon cube and cream, simmer, covered, about 10 minutes or until potatoes are soft. Remove bay leaf, blend or process mixture in several batches until smooth, stir in chives.

Place this soup and the sweet potato soup in separate jugs, pour simultaneously into serving bowls. Pull skewer through the soup for a marbled effect, as pictured.
Sweet Potato Soup: Melt butter in pan, add potato, cover, cook over medium heat 5 minutes. Stir in water, crumbled bouillon cube and cream, simmer, covered, about 10 minutes or until potato is soft. Blend or process mixture in several batches until smooth. Reheat before serving.

Serves 6.

■ Soup can be made 2 days ahead.
■ Storage: Covered, in refrigerator.
■ Freeze: Not suitable.
■ Microwave: Suitable.

ABOVE: Double Potato Soup.

BELOW: From left: Sweet Red Bell Pepper Soup; Cream of Zucchini Soup.
LEFT: Chestnut Soup.

CHESTNUT SOUP

2 tablespoons (¼ stick) butter
1 slice bacon, chopped
1 onion, chopped
1 clove garlic, minced
1 carrot, chopped
1 stalk celery, chopped
1 potato, chopped
15oz can chestnut puree
4 cups water
1 large chicken bouillon cube
¼ cup heavy cream
2 tablespoons chopped fresh chives

Heat butter in large pan, add bacon, onion and garlic, cook, stirring, until onion is soft. Add carrot, celery, potato, chestnut puree, water and crumbled bouillon cube. Simmer, covered, about 30 minutes or until vegetables are tender. Blend or process mixture in batches until smooth. Return to pan, add cream, reheat without boiling. Sprinkle with chives before serving.

Serves 6.

■ Soup can be made 2 days ahead.
■ Storage: Covered, in refrigerator.
■ Freeze: Suitable.
■ Microwave: Suitable.

SWEET RED BELL PEPPER SOUP

3 red bell peppers, halved
3 tablespoons olive oil
1 onion, chopped
1 clove garlic, minced
½ cup tomato puree
3 tablespoons tomato paste
2 cups water
2 small chicken bouillon cubes
1 teaspoon dried marjoram leaves
½ cup sour cream

Place peppers cut-side-down on baking sheet, bake in 350°F about 20 minutes or until skin blisters, cool slightly, peel away skin, chop peppers. Heat oil in pan, add onion and garlic, cook, stirring, until onion is soft. Stir in peppers, puree, paste, water and crumbled bouillon cubes. Simmer, uncovered, 30 minutes; stir in marjoram. Blend or process mixture in several batches until smooth. Return to pan, stir in sour cream, reheat without boiling.

Serves 4.

■ Soup can be made 2 days ahead; add cream just before serving.
■ Storage: Covered, in refrigerator.
■ Freeze: Without cream, suitable.
■ Microwave: Not suitable.

CREAM OF ZUCCHINI SOUP

¼ cup (½ stick) butter
1 onion, chopped
1½lb zucchini, chopped
3 tablespoons all-purpose flour
1 cup water
1 small chicken bouillon cube
1¼ cups heavy cream

Heat butter in large pan, add onion and zucchini, cook, stirring, until vegetables are soft. Stir in flour, cook, stirring, 1 minute. Remove from heat, gradually stir in water and crumbled bouillon cube, stir over high heat until mixture boils and thickens. Blend or process mixture in batches until smooth, return to pan, add cream; reheat without boiling.

Serves 4.

- Recipe can be made a day ahead.
- Storage: Covered, in refrigerator.
- Freeze: Not suitable.
- Microwave: Suitable.

RED CABBAGE AND APPLE SOUP

1 tablespoon butter
1 leek, chopped
1 clove garlic, minced
¼ cup water
3 cups (½lb) shredded red cabbage
½ cup tomato juice
1 teaspoon Worcestershire sauce
1 apple, chopped
1 potato, chopped
4 cups water, extra
1 large chicken bouillon cube
4 teaspoons chopped fresh chives

Heat butter in large pan, add leek, garlic and water, cook about 10 minutes or until leek is tender. Add cabbage, juice, sauce, apple, potato, extra water and crumbled bouillon cube, simmer, covered, about 30 minutes or until potato is soft. Blend or process mixture in batches until smooth. Reheat without boiling. Sprinkle with chives before serving.

Serves 6.

- Recipe can be made several hours ahead.
- Storage: Covered, in refrigerator.
- Freeze: Not suitable.
- Microwave: Suitable.

CREAMY CORN SOUP

1 tablespoon butter
6 green onions, chopped
3 tablespoons all-purpose flour
4 cups water
1 large vegetable bouillon cube
2 x 17oz cans creamed corn
½ cup heavy cream

Heat butter in large pan, add onions, cook, stirring, until soft. Add flour, cook, stirring, 1 minute. Remove from heat, gradually stir in water and crumbled bouillon cube, stir over high heat until mixture boils and thickens. Add corn and cream, reheat without boiling.

Serves 4.

- Recipe can be made a day ahead.
- Storage: Covered, in refrigerator.
- Freeze: Not suitable.
- Microwave: Suitable.

CELERY, POTATO AND WATERCRESS SOUP

2 tablespoons (¼ stick) butter
2 leeks, sliced
1 clove garlic, minced
4 stalks celery, chopped
4 teaspoons chopped fresh parsley
2 potatoes, chopped
4 cups water
1 small chicken bouillon cube
1 small bunch watercress

Melt butter in large pan, add leeks and garlic, cook, stirring, until leeks are soft. Stir in celery, parsley, potatoes, water and crumbled bouillon cube. Simmer, covered, 30 minutes. Add watercress, simmer until wilted. Blend or process mixture in batches until smooth. Reheat without boiling.

Serves 6.

- Recipe can be made a day ahead.
- Storage: Covered, in refrigerator.
- Freeze: Not suitable.
- Microwave: Suitable.

RIGHT: Clockwise from top: Creamy Corn Soup, Celery, Potato and Watercress Soup; Red Cabbage and Apple Soup.

CREAM OF TOMATO SOUP

¼ cup (½ stick) butter
1 onion, chopped
1 clove garlic, minced
⅓ cup all-purpose flour
2 cups milk
2 cups water
6 ripe tomatoes, peeled, chopped
3 tablespoons tomato paste
1 large vegetable bouillon cube
1 teaspoon sugar
½ cup heavy cream
4 teaspoons chopped fresh parsley

Melt butter in pan, add onion and garlic, cook, stirring, until onion is soft. Stir in flour, cook, stirring, 1 minute. Remove from heat, gradually stir in milk and water, stir over heat until mixture boils and thickens.

Add tomatoes, paste, crumbled bouillon cube and sugar, simmer, covered, 10 minutes. Blend or process mixture in batches until smooth, add cream, return to pan, reheat without boiling. Sprinkle with parsley just before serving.

Serves 6.

▨ Recipe can be made a day ahead.
▨ Storage: Covered, in refrigerator.
▨ Freeze: Not suitable.
▨ Microwave: Suitable.

VEGETABLE AND COCONUT MILK SOUP

4 teaspoons light olive oil
1 onion, chopped
2 small fresh red chili
    peppers, chopped
1 teaspoon grated fresh gingerroot
1¼ cups water
1 large chicken bouillon cube
⅔ cup canned unsweetened
    coconut milk
1 cup milk
2 teaspoons shrimp sauce
2 teaspoons light soy sauce
1 teaspoon lemon pepper
8oz can water chestnuts,
    drained, sliced
1 bunch (10 leaves) bok choy,
    chopped
14oz can straw mushrooms, drained
1 small red bell pepper,
    finely chopped

Heat oil in large pan, add onion, chili peppers and gingerroot, cook, stirring, until onion is soft. Add remaining ingredients, simmer, covered, 20 minutes.

Serves 4.

▨ Recipe can be made several
    hours ahead.
▨ Storage: Covered, in refrigerator.
▨ Freeze: Not suitable.
▨ Microwave: Suitable.

BROCCOLI AND GRUYERE SOUP WITH GARLIC CROUTONS

2 tablespoons (¼ stick) butter
2 onions, chopped
1lb broccoli, chopped
4 cups water
1 small chicken bouillon cube
⅓ cup heavy cream
½ cup grated gruyere cheese

GARLIC CROUTONS
2 slices white bread
2 tablespoons (¼ stick) butter
1 clove garlic, minced
4 teaspoons chopped fresh parsley

Heat butter in large pan, add onions, cook, stirring, until soft. Add broccoli, water and crumbled bouillon cube, simmer, covered, 30 minutes. Blend or process mixture in batches until smooth, return to pan, stir in cream, reheat without boiling. Serve sprinkled with cheese and croutons.

Garlic Croutons: Remove crusts from bread, cut bread into ½ inch cubes. Heat butter in skillet, add garlic, parsley and bread, cook, stirring, until cubes are crisp and golden.

Serves 6.

▨ Soup can be made 2 days ahead;
    add cheese just before serving.
    Croutons can be made several
    hours ahead.
▨ Storage: Covered, in refrigerator.
▨ Freeze: Without cheese, suitable.
▨ Microwave: Suitable.

LEFT: Clockwise from left: Vegetable and Coconut Milk Soup; Cream of Tomato Soup; Broccoli and Gruyere Soup with Garlic Croutons.

FRESH VEGETABLE CONSOMME

4 teaspoons whole black peppercorns
4 cloves garlic
2 bay leaves
2 stalks celery
2 carrots
1 tablespoon butter
1 leek, sliced
6 cups water
1 large vegetable bouillon cube
7oz broccoli, chopped

Tie peppercorns, garlic and bay leaves in muslin. Cut celery and carrots into short strips. Heat butter in large pan, add leek, cook, stirring, until soft. Add water, crumbled bouillon cube, muslin bag and vegetables, simmer about 5 minutes or until vegetables are just tender. Discard muslin bag.

Serves 6.

- Recipe can be made a day ahead.
- Storage: Covered, in refrigerator.
- Freeze: Not suitable.
- Microwave: Not suitable.

CURRIED PEA AND LETTUCE SOUP

2 tablespoons (¼ stick) butter
1 clove garlic, minced
1 onion, chopped
2 teaspoons curry powder
2 cups shredded lettuce
2 cups frozen green peas
3 cups water
1 large vegetable bouillon cube

Heat butter in large pan, add garlic, onion and curry powder, cook, stirring, until onion is soft. Add lettuce and peas, stir over heat until lettuce is wilted. Stir in water and crumbled bouillon cube, simmer, covered, 15 minutes. Blend or process mixture in batches until smooth. Reheat if necessary. Serve topped with sour cream and paprika, if desired.

Serves 4.

- Recipe can be made a day ahead.
- Storage: Covered, in refrigerator.
- Freeze: Suitable.
- Microwave: Suitable.

PUMPKIN SQUASH, BACON AND CARAWAY SOUP

5 slices bacon, chopped
1 large onion, chopped
2 small chicken bouillon cubes
6 cups water
1½lb pumpkin squash, chopped
1 teaspoon caraway seeds
½ cup sour cream

Add bacon and onion to large pan, cook, stirring, until onion is soft. Add crumbled bouillon cubes, water, squash and caraway seeds. Simmer, covered, about 15 minutes or until squash is tender. Blend or process squash mixture in batches until smooth. Add sour cream, reheat without boiling.

Serves 4.

- Recipe can be made 2 days ahead; add cream just before serving.
- Storage: Covered, in refrigerator.
- Freeze: Without cream, suitable.
- Microwave: Suitable.

RIGHT: Clockwise from left: Fresh Vegetable Consomme; Curried Pea and Lettuce Soup; Pumpkin Squash, Bacon and Caraway Soup.

ONION CONSOMME

¼ cup (½ stick) butter
2 large onions, chopped
2 x 14½oz cans beef consomme
4 cups water
½ cup dry red wine
1 stalk celery, chopped
½ small red bell pepper, sliced
½ small green bell pepper, sliced

Melt butter in large pan, add onions, cook, stirring, about 20 minutes or until onions are soft and well browned. Stir in consomme, water and wine, simmer, uncovered, 5 minutes. Strain mixture through fine sieve, discard onion, return consomme to pan, add celery and peppers, simmer 5 minutes.

Serves 4.

- Recipe can be made a day ahead.
- Storage: Covered, in refrigerator.
- Freeze: Not suitable.
- Microwave: Not suitable.

CREAM OF CARROT AND PARSNIP SOUP

1 tablespoon butter
3 carrots, chopped
2 parsnips, chopped
1 small onion, chopped
1 potato, chopped
4 cups water
1 large vegetable bouillon cube
¼ cup heavy cream

Melt butter in large pan, add carrots, parsnips, onion and potato. Cover, cook over low heat about 15 minutes or until vegetables are tender. Stir in water and crumbled bouillon cube, simmer, covered, 30 minutes. Blend or process mixture in batches until smooth, return soup to pan, stir in cream, reheat without boiling. Sprinkle with green onions, if desired.

Serves 4.

- Soup can be made 2 days ahead; add cream just before serving.
- Storage: Covered, in refrigerator.
- Freeze: Without cream, suitable.
- Microwave: Suitable.

CURRIED SPINACH AND COCONUT SOUP

2 tablespoons (¼ stick) butter
1 onion, finely chopped
4 teaspoons curry powder
2 potatoes, chopped
1 bunch (1¼lb) spinach, chopped
4 cups water
2 small chicken bouillon cubes
⅔ cup canned unsweetened
**   coconut cream**
½ cup heavy cream
4 teaspoons fresh lemon juice
3 tablespoons coconut

Heat butter in large pan, add onion and curry powder, cook, stirring, until onion is soft. Add potatoes and spinach, cook, stirring, until spinach is wilted. Stir in water, crumbled bouillon cubes and coconut cream. Simmer, covered, 30 minutes.

Blend or process mixture in batches until smooth. Return to pan, stir in cream and juice, reheat without boiling. Sprinkle with coconut just before serving.

Serves 4.

- Recipe can be made a day ahead.
- Storage: Covered, in refrigerator.
- Freeze: Not suitable.
- Microwave: Suitable.

ABOVE: Clockwise from left: Curried Spinach and Coconut Soup; Cream of Carrot and Parsnip Soup; Onion Consomme.

Soups

Chicken & Meat

Brimming with flavor and goodness, soups based on chicken and meat are robust pleasures to enjoy, especially on winter evenings. Serve them with a meal or to compensate for a light main course. They are satisfying snacks too.

HEARTY POTATO, BACON AND ONION SOUP

4 slices bacon, chopped
2 tablespoons (¼ stick) butter
3 onions, sliced
3 tablespoons all-purpose flour
4 cups water
1 large vegetable bouillon cube
4 potatoes, chopped
2 egg yolks
8oz container sour cream
4 teaspoons chopped fresh parsley

Cook bacon in large pan until lightly browned, add butter and onions, cook, stirring, until onions are soft. Add flour, cook, stirring, 1 minute. Remove from heat, gradually add water, crumbled bouillon cube and potatoes, simmer, uncovered about 10 minutes or until potatoes are cooked. Gradually stir in combined egg yolks and sour cream, reheat without boiling. Stir in parsley.

Serves 6.

■ Recipe can be made a day ahead; add cream mixture and parsley just before serving.
■ Storage: Covered, in refrigerator.
■ Freeze: Not suitable.
■ Microwave: Not suitable.

BELOW: Hearty Potato, Bacon and Onion Soup.

CREAMY LAMB SOUP WITH MUSHROOMS

4 lean lamb sirloin chops
1 cup milk
1½ cups water
3 tablespoons butter
1 onion, finely chopped
5oz button mushrooms, sliced
¼ cup all-purpose flour
1 large beef bouillon cube
1¼ cups heavy cream

Remove fat from chops. Heat milk and water in pan, add chops. Simmer about 15 minutes or until chops are cooked. Remove chops, cut meat finely. Strain and reserve liquid.

Melt butter in pan, add onion, cook, stirring, until soft. Add mushrooms, cook, stirring, 2 minutes.

Blend flour with a little of the reserved liquid, add to pan with lamb, remaining liquid and crumbled bouillon cube, stir over high heat until mixture boils and thickens. Add cream, reheat, without boiling, before serving.

Serves 4.

- Recipe can be made 3 days ahead; add cream just before serving.
- Storage: Covered, in refrigerator.
- Freeze: Not suitable.
- Microwave: Suitable.

PORK AND PEARL ONION SOUP

6 cups water
1 large chicken bouillon cube
12 pearl onions, sliced
1lb pork tenderloins, sliced
8oz can sliced bamboo
  shoots, drained
3 tablespoons liquid dashi
4 teaspoons grated fresh gingerroot
4 green onions, sliced
1 small carrot

Combine water, crumbled bouillon cube and onions in large pan, simmer, covered, 10 minutes. Add pork, bamboo shoots, dashi, gingerroot and green onions, simmer, covered, about 5 minutes or until pork is just cooked. Cut carrot into strips; boil, steam or microwave carrot until just tender. Serve soup with carrot.

Serves 6.

- Recipe can be made a day ahead.
- Storage: Covered, in refrigerator.
- Freeze: Not suitable.
- Microwave: Not suitable.

CREAM OF CHICKEN AND ALMOND SOUP

5 cups water
2 chicken breast halves
1 onion, chopped
4 whole cloves
1 teaspoon cumin seeds
½ teaspoon dried thyme leaves
8 black peppercorns
2 potatoes, chopped
2 tablespoons (¼ stick) butter
1 clove garlic, minced
1 onion, chopped, extra
¼ cup slivered almonds
⅔ cup heavy cream
¼ teaspoon ground coriander

Add water to large pan, add chicken, onion, cloves, cumin, thyme and peppercorns, simmer, covered, 1 hour. Remove chicken from broth, cool, refrigerate. Strain broth into large bowl, cool, refrigerate overnight.

Next day, remove fat from broth. Remove and discard skin and bones from chicken, coarsely chop chicken.

Add broth to large pan, bring to boil, add potatoes, simmer, covered, about 15 minutes or until tender. Blend or process mixture in batches until smooth; return to pan. Heat butter in pan, add garlic, extra onion and almonds, cook, stirring, over medium heat until almonds are lightly browned. Blend or process almond mixture and chicken meat until well combined. Add to potato mixture, bring to boil, remove from heat, stir in cream and coriander, reheat mixture without boiling.

Serves 4.

- Recipe can be made a day ahead; add cream just before serving.
- Storage: Covered, in refrigerator.
- Freeze: Not suitable.
- Microwave: Not suitable.

BACON AND GARLIC TOMATO SOUP

4 teaspoons olive oil
1 large onion, chopped
3 cloves garlic, minced
1 teaspoon grated fresh gingerroot
3 slices bacon, chopped
½ teaspoon chili powder
2 x 14½ oz cans tomatoes
4 teaspoons tomato paste
1 small chicken bouillon cube
1 cup water
⅓ cup dry red wine

Heat oil in large pan, add onion, garlic, gingerroot and bacon, cook, stirring, until bacon is cooked. Stir in chili powder, undrained crushed tomatoes, paste, crumbled bouillon cube, water and wine. Simmer, uncovered, 5 minutes. Blend or process mixture in batches until well combined. Return to pan, reheat before serving.

Serves 4.

- Recipe can be made a day ahead.
- Storage: Covered, in refrigerator.
- Freeze: Suitable.
- Microwave: Suitable.

ABOVE: From top: Cream of Chicken and Almond Soup; Bacon and Garlic Tomato Soup.
LEFT: From top: Creamy Lamb Soup with Mushrooms; Pork and Pearl Onion Soup.

Soups

Cold

Light, fresh and summery. These soups are perfect before a heavier main course. There are delightful, palate-cleansing fruit soups among other great flavors. Always cool cooked mixtures to room temperature before refrigerating.

ABOVE: Chilled Leek and Beet Consomme.
RIGHT: From top: Cantaloupe Cream Soup;
Cherry, Lemon and Cinnamon Soup.

CHILLED LEEK AND BEET CONSOMME

4 teaspoons light olive oil
14oz leeks, chopped
4 cups water
3 large (1lb) beets, chopped
2 cloves garlic
1½ cups fresh orange juice
4 teaspoons red wine vinegar

Heat oil in large pan, add leeks, cook, stirring, until soft. Add remaining ingredients, simmer, covered, 1 hour, strain mixture into large bowl. Cool, cover, refrigerate consomme several hours before serving.

Serves 4.

■ Recipe can be made a day ahead.
■ Storage: Covered, in refrigerator.
■ Freeze: Not suitable.
■ Microwave: Not suitable.

CHERRY, LEMON AND CINNAMON SOUP

1 cup water
½ cup superfine sugar
2 x 16½oz cans pitted dark sweet cherries, drained
¼ cup Kirsch
⅓ cup fresh lemon juice
1 cinnamon stick
⅓ cup sour cream
½ teaspoon ground cinnamon

Combine water and sugar in pan, stir over heat, without boiling, until sugar is dissolved. Blend or process cherries until smooth. Add cherries, liqueur, juice and cinnamon stick to pan, simmer, covered, 5 minutes. Remove cinnamon stick. Pour mixture into bowl, cool, cover, refrigerate several hours. Serve topped with sour cream and cinnamon.

Serves 6.

■ Recipe can be made 2 days ahead.
■ Storage: Covered, in refrigerator.
■ Freeze: Not suitable.
■ Microwave: Not suitable.

CANTALOUPE CREAM SOUP

1 cantaloupe, chopped
½ cup white grape juice
4 teaspoons fresh lime juice
1 tablespoon grated orange zest
½ cup heavy cream

Blend cantaloupe and juices in batches until smooth. Pour mixture into bowl, stir in zest, cover, refrigerate. Add cream just before serving.

Serves 4.

■ Recipe can be made several hours ahead.
■ Storage: Covered, in refrigerator.
■ Freeze: Not suitable.

CARROT AND CILANTRO SOUP

2 tablespoons (¼ stick) butter
1 large onion, chopped
1 teaspoon grated fresh gingerroot
4 cups water
2 small chicken bouillon cubes
4 carrots, chopped
4 teaspoons chopped fresh cilantro

Heat butter in large pan, add onion and gingerroot, cook, stirring, until onion is soft. Add water, crumbled bouillon cubes and carrots, simmer, covered, about 10 minutes or until carrots are tender. Blend or process mixture in batches until smooth. Pour mixture into bowl, stir in cilantro, cool, cover; refrigerate several hours before serving.

Serves 4.

- Recipe can be made 2 days ahead.
- Storage: Covered, in refrigerator.
- Freeze: Suitable.
- Microwave: Suitable.

COOL CUCUMBER SOUP

6 cups water
1 large chicken bouillon cube
2 green onions, chopped
2 cloves garlic, minced
1 tablespoon drained green peppercorns
2 green cucumbers, thinly sliced
8oz can whole water chestnuts, drained, sliced
¼ cup white wine vinegar
2 cups roughly chopped watercress
4 teaspoons icing sugar

Combine water, crumbled bouillon cube, onions, garlic and peppercorns in large pan, simmer, covered, 10 minutes. Cool, pour into large bowl, cover, refrigerate several hours. Stir in cucumbers, water chestnuts, vinegar, watercress and sugar.

Serves 6.

- Recipe can be made a day ahead.
- Storage: Covered, in refrigerator.
- Freeze: Not suitable.
- Microwave: Suitable.

LEFT: From top: Carrot and Cilantro Soup; Cool Cucumber Soup.
RIGHT: From left: Pumpkin Squash and Coconut Soup; Cauliflower and Spinach Soup.

CAULIFLOWER AND SPINACH SOUP

4 teaspoons olive oil
1 onion, chopped
1lb cauliflower, chopped
1 bunch (1¼lb) spinach, chopped
2½ cups water
1 small chicken bouillon cube
1¼ cups milk
⅛ teaspoon cayenne pepper
2oz oyster mushrooms, sliced

Heat oil in large pan, add onion, cook, stirring, until soft. Add cauliflower, spinach, water, crumbled bouillon cube, milk and pepper, simmer, covered, about 20 minutes or until cauliflower is tender. Blend or process mixture in batches until smooth, stir in mushrooms, cool, cover, refrigerate several hours before serving.

Serves 4.

■ Recipe can be made a day ahead.
■ Storage: Covered, in refrigerator.
■ Freeze: Not suitable.
■ Microwave: Suitable.

PUMPKIN SQUASH AND COCONUT SOUP

1 tablespoon butter
1 clove garlic, minced
1lb pumpkin squash, chopped
4 cups water
1 large vegetable bouillon cube
⅔ cup canned unsweetened coconut cream

Heat butter and garlic in large pan. Stir in squash, water and crumbled bouillon cube, simmer, covered, about 25 minutes or until squash is tender. Remove from heat, cool.

Blend or process squash mixture in batches until smooth, place in bowl, stir in coconut cream, refrigerate several hours before serving.

Serves 6.

■ Recipe can be made 2 days ahead.
■ Storage: Covered, in refrigerator.
■ Freeze: Suitable.
■ Microwave: Suitable.

Soups

Pasta, Noodles, Beans, etc

The delicious variety of thick and nutritious soups in this section are made even more satisfying with the addition of pasta, noodles and beans. For contrast, the elegant chicken consomme is light though subtly enhanced with noodles.

CHUNKY CHORIZO SAUSAGE AND BEAN SOUP

2 tablespoons (¼ stick) butter
1 onion, finely chopped
1 clove garlic, minced
3 chorizo sausages, chopped
3 tablespoons all-purpose flour
1 cup milk
1¾ cups water
1 large vegetable bouillon cube
10oz canned white kidney beans (cannellini), drained
¼ cup heavy cream
2 teaspoons chopped fresh oregano
2 teaspoons chopped fresh basil

Melt butter in pan, add onion, garlic and sausages, cook, stirring, 5 minutes. Stir in flour, cook, stirring, 2 minutes. Remove from heat, gradually stir in combined milk, water and crumbled bouillon cube. Stir over high heat until mixture boils and thickens. Add beans, cream and herbs, stir until heated through.

Serves 4.

- Recipe can made 2 days ahead.
- Storage: Covered, in refrigerator.
- Freeze: Suitable.
- Microwave: Suitable.

SPEEDY MINESTRONE

2 tablespoons (¼ stick) butter
1 onion, thinly sliced
1 clove garlic, minced
2 slices bacon, chopped
1 stalk celery, chopped
1 carrot, chopped
14½oz can tomatoes
8¾oz can red kidney beans, drained
3 cups water
1 small chicken bouillon cube
⅓ cup pasta twists
¼ cup grated Parmesan cheese

Heat butter in large pan, add onion, garlic and bacon, cook, stirring, until onion is soft. Add celery and carrot, cook, stirring, 2 minutes. Stir in undrained crushed tomatoes, beans, water, crumbled bouillon cube and pasta. Simmer, covered, 30 minutes. Serve topped with cheese.

Serves 6.

- Recipe can be made 2 days ahead.
- Storage: Covered, in refrigerator.
- Freeze: Suitable.
- Microwave: Suitable.

RIGHT: From left: Chunky Chorizo Sausage and Bean Soup; Speedy Minestrone.

CURRIED LENTIL AND VEGETABLE SOUP

3 tablespoons olive oil
1 tablespoon curry powder
1 onion, chopped
6 cups water
1 large chicken bouillon cube
4 teaspoons tomato paste
1 cup red lentils
1/4lb broccoli, chopped
1 small carrot, chopped
1 stalk celery, chopped
1 small zucchini, chopped

Heat oil in large pan, add curry powder and onion, cook, stirring, until onion is soft. Add water, crumbled bouillon cube and paste, bring to boil, reduce heat. Add lentils, simmer, covered, 15 minutes. Add broccoli, carrot, celery and zucchini, simmer, covered, about 15 minutes or until vegetables and lentils are tender.

Serves 6.

■ Recipe can be made 2 days ahead.
■ Storage: Covered, in refrigerator.
■ Freeze: Suitable.
■ Microwave: Suitable.

CORN AND NOODLE SOUP

4 cups water
2 small chicken bouillon cubes
2oz vermicelli egg noodles
2 green onions, chopped
1/4 cup bamboo shoots, finely sliced
1/2 red bell pepper, sliced
1 slice (1oz) cooked ham, sliced
2 teaspoons light soy sauce
1 tablespoon dry sherry
1 teaspoon grated fresh gingerroot
8 3/4oz can whole-kernel corn, drained
1/2 cup bean sprouts
2 tablespoons cornstarch
3 tablespoons water, extra

Combine water and crumbled bouillon cubes in large pan, bring to boil. Add noodles, onions, bamboo shoots, pepper, ham, sauce, sherry and gingerroot. Simmer, covered, 5 minutes. Stir in corn and sprouts. Stir in blended cornstarch and extra water, stir over high heat until soup boils and thickens.

Serves 4.

■ Recipe can be made several hours ahead.
■ Storage: Covered, in refrigerator.
■ Freeze: Not suitable.
■ Microwave: Not suitable.

CHICKEN VERMICELLI CONSOMME

4 teaspoons light olive oil
1lb chicken wings
1 onion, chopped
1 carrot, chopped
1 stalk celery, chopped
2 bay leaves
12 cups water
2 egg whites
1/4lb ground veal
1 1/2oz vermicelli egg noodles
4 teaspoons chopped fresh chives
1 small fresh red chili pepper, finely chopped

Heat oil in large pan, add chicken, onion, carrot and celery, cook, stirring, until chicken is browned. Add bay leaves and water; simmer, covered, 2 hours; cool. Strain broth into bowl. Discard chicken and vegetables. Refrigerate several hours or overnight. Remove fat from broth. Return broth to pan, boil, uncovered, until broth is reduced by about two-thirds, clarify broth to complete consomme.

To clarify broth: Place 1 cup broth in large bowl, whisk in unbeaten egg whites and veal. Bring remaining broth to boil in pan, whisk into veal and egg white mixture in a thin steam. Return mixture to pan, whisk over heat until mixture comes to

simmer, simmer gently 15 minutes. Strain mixture slowly through a sieve which has been lined with 2 layers of muslin or absorbent paper; discard veal mixture.

Add vermicelli to pan of boiling water, boil, uncovered, until vermicelli is tender, drain, rinse under cold water. Add vermicelli, chives and chili to consomme, reheat before serving.

Serves 4.

- Chicken broth can be made 2 days ahead; clarify broth close to serving.
- Storage: Covered, in refrigerator.
- Freeze: Broth suitable.
- Microwave: Not suitable.

ABOVE: From left: Corn and Noodle Soup; Chicken Vermicelli Consomme.
LEFT: Curried Lentil and Vegetable Soup.

Glossary

Some terms, names and alternatives are included here to help everyone understand and use our recipes perfectly.

BOK CHOY (Chinese chard): remove and discard stems, use leaves and young tender parts of stems. It requires only a short cooking time.

BOUILLON CUBE: a small cube is equivalent to 1 teaspoon powdered bouillon, a large cube is equivalent to 2 teaspoons powdered bouillon.

BREAD CRUMBS

Fresh: use 1 or 2 day old white or whole-wheat bread made into crumbs by grating, blending or processing.

Packaged unseasoned: use commercially packaged unseasoned bread crumbs.

BUTTER: use salted or unsalted butter, or use margarine of your choice.

CHICKEN

Tenderloins: this is the strip of meat found on the underside of the breast. If unavailable, use sliced, boneless, skinless breast halves.

CHILI

Fresh: use rubber gloves when handling fresh chili peppers as they can burn your skin. The seeds are the hottest part; remove them if you want to reduce the heat in a recipe. Use ½ teaspoon chili powder instead of 1 small fresh chili pepper.

Powder: ground dried chili peppers.

Sauce: we used the hot Asian variety.

CHINESE MIXED PICKLES: consists of a variety of fruit and vegetables preserved in vinegar, sugar and salt. The jar we used contained gingerroot, green onions, papaya, cucumbers, carrots, chili and pears.

CHORIZO SAUSAGES: Spanish and Mexican highly spiced pork sausages seasoned with garlic, cayenne pepper, chili, etc. They are ready to eat when bought. If unavailable, use a spicy salami.

COCONUT CREAM AND MILK: we used unsweetened coconut cream and milk available in cans in supermarkets and Asian food stores. Coconut milk can be substituted for the cream, although it is not as thick and creamy.

COINTREAU: an orange-flavored liqueur.

CREAM

Light sour: a less dense commercially cultured soured cream; do not substitute this for sour cream.

Sour: a thick commercially cultured soured cream.

DASHI: is a basic fish and seaweed broth responsible for the distinctive flavor of Japanese food. It is made from dried bonito flakes and konbu. Instant dashi, a good substitute, is readily available from Asian food stores.

FLOUR

Self-rising flour: substitute all-purpose flour and double-acting baking powder in the proportion of 1 cup all-purpose flour to 2 teaspoons double-acting baking powder; sift together several times.

FROGS LEGS: available from specialty food stores.

GARAM MASALA: usually a mixture of cardamom, cinnamon, cloves, coriander, cumin and nutmeg, available from Asian food stores.

GINGERROOT

Glace gingerroot: crystallized gingerroot can be substituted; rinse off the sugar with warm water, dry gingerroot well before using.

GRAND MARNIER: an orange-flavored liqueur.

HERBS

Ground: use powdered form.

Dried leaves: use dehydrated herb leaves.

Fresh: if unavailable, use a quarter of dried leaves instead of the fresh; for example use 1 teaspoon dried basil leaves as a substitute for 4 teaspoons chopped fresh basil. This is not recommended when more than a tablespoon of fresh herbs is to be substituted in the recipe.

HOISIN SAUCE: is a thick sweet Chinese barbeque sauce made from salted black beans, onion and garlic.

JALAPENO CHILI PEPPERS: imported, canned, pickled, hot chili peppers. Store any leftover chili peppers in their liquid in an airtight container in the refrigerator.

LETTUCE: we used mostly iceberg, radicchio, red leaf and Boston lettuce.

LUMPFISH CAVIAR: this is not a true caviar, but an economical substitute; orange and black varieties are available.

MARSALA: a sweet fortified wine.

MUSHROOMS

Chinese dried: unique in flavor; soak in hot water, covered, 20 minutes, drain. Remove and discard stems, use caps.

Oyster: these are also known as abalone mushrooms; small fresh cultivated mushrooms.

Straw: available in cans (champignons can be substituted; these are small cultivated canned mushrooms).

MUSTARD, SEEDED: a French style of mustard with crushed mustard seeds.

OIL: we used a light olive oil in our recipes unless otherwise stated.

OYSTER-FLAVORED SAUCE: a rich brown bottled sauce made from oysters, cooked in salt and soy sauce.

PIMIENTOS: canned or bottled whole or halved bell peppers.

PLUM SAUCE: a dipping sauce which consists of plums preserved in vinegar, sweetened with sugar and flavored with chili peppers and spices.

PORK, BARBEQUED: roasted Chinese red pork available from Asian food stores and specialty food stores.

POTATO, DRY INSTANT: flaked or powdered dried potato which makes quick mashed potato; it is available from supermarkets.

PROSCIUTTO: uncooked, unsmoked ham cured in salt, usually bought in very thin slices.

QUAIL EGGS: available from specialty food stores.

RICE, BASMATI: a light-textured, delicately flavored slender grain rice; white long-grain rice can be substituted.

SAKE: Japan's rice wine, is used in cooking, marinating and as part of dipping sauces. If unavailable, dry sherry, vermouth or brandy can be used.

SAMBAL OELEK (also sambal ulek): is a paste made from ground chili peppers and salt, can be used as an ingredient or an accompaniment.

SCALLOPS, SEA: we used sea scallops with the orange coral attached.

SESAME OIL: made from roasted, crushed white sesame seeds, is an aromatic golden-colored oil with a nutty flavor. Use in small quantities as a flavoring. It is not the same as the sesame oil sold in natural food stores.

It can be bought in supermarkets and Asian food stores.

SHRIMP SAUCE: a powerful mix of dried shrimp and salt; available from Asian food stores.

SNOW PEAS: also known as Chinese pea pods, they are small flat pods with barely formed peas; they are eaten whole. You need only to top and tail young pods, older ones need stringing. Cook for a short time (about 30 seconds) either by stir-frying or blanching, or until just tender.

SOY SAUCE: made from fermented soya beans; available in light and dark varieties. The light sauce is generally used with white meat dishes, and the darker with red meat dishes. Dark soy is generally used for color, and light for flavor. Light soy sauce contains more salt.

SUN-DRIED TOMATOES: are dried tomatoes sometimes bottled in oil; drain well before using.

TAHINI (SESAME PASTE): made from crushed sesame seeds.

TAMARIND SAUCE: is made from the acid-tasting fruit of the tamarind tree. If unavailable, soak about 1oz dried tamarind in a cup of water, stand 10 minutes. Squeeze the pulp as dry as possible and use the flavored water.

TERIYAKI SAUCE: based on light Japanese soy sauce; contains sugar, spices and vinegar.

TIMBALE: a dish similar to a souffle or custard mold which is round in shape with straight or sloping sides.

TOASTING

Nuts: can be toasted in the oven; spread them evenly onto a baking sheet, toast in 350°F oven about 5 minutes or until lightly browned.

Sesame seeds: toast evenly by stirring over heat in a heavy-based skillet; the natural oils will brown the seeds.

TOMATO PUREE: You can use canned tomato puree or a puree of fresh, ripe tomatoes made by blending or processing the amount required.

WINE: we used good dry red and dry white wines.

WINE VINEGAR: made from wine and is often flavored with herbs, spices, fruit, etc.

WORCESTERSHIRE SAUCE: a dark piquant sauce commonly used in the UK.

White wine Worcestershire sauce: a pale Worcestershire sauce, based on white wine.

YEAST: allow 2 teaspoons (¼oz) active dry yeast to each ½oz fresh yeast, if substituting.

MAKE YOUR OWN BROTH

BEEF BROTH

4lb meaty beef bones
2 onions
2 stalks celery, chopped
2 carrots, chopped
3 bay leaves
2 teaspoons black peppercorns
20 cups water
12 cups water, extra

Place bones and unpeeled chopped onions in roasting pan. Bake, uncovered, in 400°F oven about 1 hour or until bones and onions are well browned. Transfer bones and onions to large pan, add celery, carrots, bay leaves, peppercorns and water, simmer, uncovered, 3 hours. Add extra water, simmer, uncovered, further 1 hour; strain.

Makes about 10 cups.

- Broth can be made 4 days ahead.
- Storage: Covered, in refrigerator.
- Freeze: Suitable.
- Microwave: Not suitable.

CHICKEN BROTH

4lb chicken bones
2 onions, chopped
2 stalks celery, chopped
2 carrots, chopped
3 bay leaves
2 teaspoons black peppercorns
20 cups water

Combine all ingredients in large pan, simmer, uncovered, 2 hours; strain.

Makes about 10 cups.

- Broth can be made 4 days ahead.
- Storage: Covered, in refrigerator.
- Freeze: Suitable.
- Microwave: Not suitable.

FISH BROTH

3lb fish bones
12 cups water
1 onion, chopped
2 stalks celery, chopped
2 bay leaves
1 teaspoon black peppercorns

Combine all ingredients in large pan, simmer, uncovered, 20 minutes; strain.

Makes about 10 cups.

- Broth can be made 4 days ahead.
- Storage: Covered, in refrigerator.
- Freeze: Suitable.
- Microwave: Not suitable.

VEGETABLE BROTH

1 large carrot, chopped
1 large parsnip, chopped
2 onions, chopped
6 stalks celery, chopped
4 bay leaves
2 teaspoons black peppercorns
12 cups water

Combine all ingredients in large pan, simmer, uncovered, 1½ hours; strain.

Makes about 5 cups.

- Broth can be made 4 days ahead.
- Storage: Covered, in refrigerator.
- Freeze: Suitable.
- Microwave: Not suitable.

Index

CUP AND SPOON MEASUREMENTS

To ensure accuracy in your recipes use standard measuring equipment.

a) 8 fluid oz cup for measuring liquids.

b) a graduated set of four cups – measuring 1 cup, half, third and quarter cup – for items such as flour, sugar etc.
When measuring in these fractional cups level off at the brim.

c) a graduated set of five spoons: tablespoon (½ fluid oz liquid capacity), teaspoon, half, quarter amd eighth teaspoons.
All spoon measurements are level.

We have used large eggs with an average weight of 2oz each in all our recipes.

Home Library
Salads
Sensational recipes for all occasions

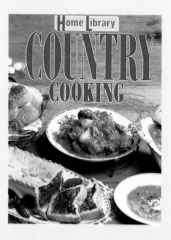

Home Library
COUNTRY COOKING

Home Library
Healthy Heart Cookbook

Home Library
VEGETARIAN COOKING

THE BEST SEAFOOD RECIPES
Home Library

Home Library
Italian COOKING CLASS COOKBOOK

Home Library
CHICKEN COOKBOOK
PLUS duck, quail, turkey, goose and more

Home Library
PASTA COOKBOOK
More than 170 recipes

Home Library
CHINESE COOKING CLASS COOKBOOK

Home Library
STARTERS AND SOUPS

Home Library
BEGINNERS' COOKBOOK

Home Library
FINGER FOOD
Best ever party food
Tempting hot and cold savouries
Do ahead and freezing tips